KENT CHR**ONICLES** OF
CATASTROPHE & DISASTER

Phil Mason

COUNTRYSIDE BOOKS
NEWBURY BERKSHIRE

First published 2008
© Phil Mason, 2008

COUNTRYSIDE BOOKS
3 Catherine Road
Newbury, Berkshire

To view our complete range of books,
please visit us at
www.countrysidebooks.co.uk

ISBN 978 1 84674 123 4

Designed by Peter Davies, Nautilus Design
Produced through MRM Associates Ltd., Reading
Typeset by Jean Cussons Typesetting, Diss, Norfolk
Printed by Information Press, Oxford

All material for the manufacture of this book
was sourced from sustainable forests

CONTENTS

INTRODUCTION   6

1 WAR AND BATTLE – ANCIENT TIMES   7

▇ *The first invasions of Britain – the Roman arrivals*
▇ *Gruesome tokens of a bloodbath – the St Brice's Day
massacre* ▇ *Feeling it in the bones – the unfortunate
Archbishop Alphege* ▇ *A macabre and mysterious
collection – the Hythe ossuary* ▇ *The expulsion of the
Jews* ▇ *Revenge for Hastings – the first Battle of Sandwich*
▇ *The origins of a mourning tradition – the second Battle
of Sandwich* ▇ *The last invasion of England*

2 WAR AND BATTLE – MODERN TIMES   22

▇ *Britain's first air raid* ▇ *The German invasion tunnel
scare* ▇ *The train that shot down a plane* ▇ *Kent on the
front line again – doodlebugs and shells from France*

3 ACCIDENTS   30

▇ *Young lives wiped out in Kent's worst road accident*
▇ *The Thames' worst catastrophe – the* Princess Alice
disaster ▇ *A holiday fire tragedy – the Gillingham 'fireman's
wedding' inferno* ▇ *A Dickens of a scrape – the Staplehurst
rail disaster* ▇ *A wartime catastrophe – the Faversham
munitions factory blast* ▇ *When the Navy had to sink its
own ship – the* Glatton *disaster* ▇ *The loss of the* Truculent
▇ *The birth of the Goodwin Sands – myth and mystery*

4 UNSOLVED MYSTERIES 50

■ *Britain's greatest lost treasure – the Becket shrine* ■ *A Victorian tragedy – the Franklin expedition* ■ *Britain's worst mass murderer? – four wartime ship explosions* ■ *The mysterious death of a flying legend – the crash of Amy Johnson* ■ *Mystery death of a musician – the unknown fate of Glenn Miller* ■ *More mysteries of the Channel – shipping enigmas* ■ *Unnatural phenomena – fear-inducing occurrences* ■ *The first UFO? – mass panic in the Medway*

5 WICKED NATURE 66

■ *Kent earthquakes* ■ *Weird and wicked weather* ■ *The deepest freeze* ■ *The driest drought* ■ *Wicked storms* ■ *The weirdest weather year* ■ *Summer ice storms* ■ *THE Great Storm* ■ *Kent's tornado* ■ *The North Sea surge – the floods of 1953*

6 ENGINEERING DISASTERS 75

■ *Would he have been the first man to fly an aeroplane? – Percy Pilcher* ■ *The first parachute death* ■ *The first safety precautions for the Goodwin Sands* ■ *Building a house on sand – the misplaced Goodwin Sands lighthouse* ■ *A disastrous testing of a new weapon of war – torpedoes at Herne Bay* ■ *The defence that was never needed – the Royal Military Canal*

7 CATASTROPHIC CHARACTERS 89

■ *The Russians are coming! – the manic visit of Peter the Great* ■ *Faversham's disastrous royal relic – King Stephen, England's worst king* ■ *The town that didn't read the script – obstructing the Glorious Revolution* ■ *Kent's most notorious assassination – the death of Becket* ■ *The extreme huntsman – an animal killer extraordinaire* ■ *The last British soldier to fall in action on English soil* ■ *The crazy men in their flying machine – the 'hopping Yank'*

8 END ODDITIES   105

■ *A ghostly tragedy replays itself – the* Lady Luvibund *mystery* ■ *Ahoy – fancy meeting you here! – a coincidental accident* ■ *'Fire, help – send a telegram' – Kent's strangest document?* ■ *The longest fire* ■ *Personal disasters* ■ *If at first you don't succeed (1)* ■ *If at first you don't succeed (2)* ■ *Death in a bucket* ■ *Run over by a train 12 times* ■ *A miraculous escape*

———————◄●●►———————

A NOTE ON BOUNDARIES

Kent has been fortunate in suffering few boundary changes in its history. All the events described in this book occurred within the boundaries of Kent as they were at the time of the event, though some may lie outside the county today.

———————◄●●►———————

Note: Illustrations used in this book are understood to be public domain images under relevant copyright laws. Every effort has been made to secure permissions. Inadvertent errors will gladly be corrected in any future edition upon notification. Meanwhile, grateful acknowledgement is given to the Medway Archives & Local Studies Centre, Strood, for permission to use the illustrations on pages 31, 32, 37, 38.

INTRODUCTION

■ *I came back through a country the best cultivated of any that in my life I had anywhere seene, every field lying as even as a bowling greene and the fences, plantations and husbandrie in such admirable order, as infinitely delighted me.*

SO WROTE JOHN EVELYN in his diary in March 1672 as he travelled through the county. Order. Neatness. Composure. The name, Kent, and its ubiquitous marque 'the garden of England' probably conjures up for most the same warm reassuring aura of tranquillity, of serene peacefulness, of man and nature in harmony.

Kent Chronicles of Catastrophe and Disaster gives the other side of the story. Here we delve into the chaotic history of the county, recent and far gone, to trace a thread of turmoil, anarchy and woe that lies behind Kent's placid façade.

Many of the events that follow have been lost to current memory, and will surprise and perhaps shock the modern reader. Many involved hundreds or thousands of deaths, often with the fate of the country in the balance; others are very individual tragedies, some with national significance.

We have drawn our net wide to capture a rich array of misfortune – the misery of war, natural disasters, accidents, twists of fate and the mysterious. We touch on the thwarted hopes of individuals for whom, had fate not intervened, greater fame may well have awaited in the future. We also discover the just plain odd, with a concluding miscellany of scarcely believable incidents.

This is not a dry chronology, nor does it pretend to be a comprehensive account of every terrible event. We have chosen to re-shine the spotlight on the stranger, more curious and lesser known side of Kent history. Many of the episodes recounted are long lost in the past. A heritage of daunting suffering and calamity has faded out of our consciousness. In *Kent Chronicles of Catastrophe and Disaster* we aim to restore to memory these fragments of our history.

Phil Mason

WAR AND BATTLE
– ANCIENT TIMES

THE FIRST INVASIONS OF BRITAIN

■ *Geography has placed Kent in the unfortunate position of being the most favoured route for an invader from the Continent. Down the centuries, Kent folk have been required to absorb on their nation's behalf the early blows from invading armies. The first in recorded history showed, like many to follow, that the county's people were far from being a walkover.*

THE ROMAN INVASION OF BRITAIN began in spectacular anti-climax on 27 August 55 BC when Julius Caesar's fleet of eighty ships carrying 10,000 troops of the famed 7th and 10th Legions arrived at dawn off the Kent coast and to their dismay saw the cliffs lined with waiting Britons. Caesar spent most of the day moored safely offshore until he had composed himself for a landing. After firing slings, arrows and crossbows at the natives all day, the first Romans struggled onto the beach between five and six o'clock that evening.

Historians have argued ceaselessly and largely fruitlessly over the centuries about where exactly Caesar landed (and indeed when: there are various claims based on tide movements for both the day before and the day before that). Theories have ranged from Thanet in the north through Hythe to as far south as Pevensey Bay in Sussex. The strongest claim and the likeliest site is near Deal and there is a commemorative plaque to this effect on the seafront at Walmer.

This was not, as is often thought, the occasion of Caesar's famous *Veni, Vidi, Vici* cry of triumph (that was to be uttered eight years later

CAESAR'S FIRST INVASION WAS A SORRY MISJUDGEMENT. HE DID NOT EXPECT
SUCH RESISTANCE. IN THIS FANCIFUL DEPICTION, HIS BODY LANGUAGE SUGGESTS
'WHAT'S GOING ON HERE?'

at a victory in Asia Minor); in fact, for Rome's greatest military organiser, the expedition was one of his worst failures. He stayed just 25 days and never ventured more than a few miles inland.

It had been a snap decision to cross the English Channel and the idea had generated no enthusiasm amongst his generals. Despite being ordered to prepare for the expedition, his entire cavalry contingent were so convinced it was a bad idea that they slowed their arrangements to such an extent that they managed to avoid sailing with the fleet. Then bad weather intervened to prevent them from catching up. Caesar would have to make do without any mounted support. It was to prove fatal to the mission.

Caesar had hopelessly misjudged the scale of the British defences and the whole operation nearly foundered because of bad weather. A storm blew most of the fleet from their moorings a few days after the invasion. Even on a very personal scale, the episode was covered in ignominy. There is a story, legendary it may be, that as he himself landed on the beach he slipped and fell on his face, getting a mouthful of sand as his welcome to Britain. As he sat in his tent reflecting during those days on the beach at Deal, he may have started to agree that it seemed all a rather bad idea – 'I came, I saw, I concurred!'

His short forays into the hinterland revealed an unsuspected level of technical capacity among the local tribesfolk. He encountered for the first time an ancient weapon of war that had long ceased to be part of current armouries on the Continent – the war chariot. Thousands of years earlier, it had been a highly effective weapon of ancient Middle East civilisations, but contrary to popular myth, by Roman times the chariot had been relegated to entirely ceremonial use. The Ancient Britons, however, used it as a devastating weapon for hit and run guerrilla raids on the invaders' camps and slow-moving armies on the march.

In all, Caesar barely made any advance from his beachhead. He fought three skirmishes to little effect, put on a brave face, and returned to Gaul. He had been bettered tactically for the first time in his career, failed to secure any cession of territory and did not even carry back any booty.

But the allure of this mysterious northern land could not be resisted. Eleven months later, in July 54 BC, he came back, this time with close to 800 ships, 21,000 foot soldiers and 2,000 cavalry. And this time he fought his way across Kent to the Medway.

Caesar's success is often put down to his own use of a strange weapon never before seen by his opponent – an elephant, operating as his main battle weapon from which archers fired volleys of arrows. No Britons had ever seen such a beast before. Nevertheless, it still took Caesar two days to cross the river. No previous battle in the history of the Roman army had lasted more than a single day.

He marched on the Thames which he crossed probably at

Shepperton to the west of London, skirted the city and got as far as Hertfordshire before retiring, harried every step of the way by the guerrilla tactics of the Britons. It was these unorthodox tactics that finally defeated the more regimented and unimaginative Roman military mind, one more used to succeeding through sheer weight of force against a static opponent. Caesar was reduced again to exasperation and after little more than two months in Britain he retreated, taking every soldier with him. Britain, and Kent, would remain unmolested for another hundred years before the Romans tried again – in AD 43 – and stayed.

▓ *The Romans would stay for 350 years, a period largely of peace. Some 40 years after their departure, the first permanent settlers – Jutes from Jutland – were brought from the Continent by the emerging British kings to defend the eastern and southern coasts. Two, perhaps mythical, brothers Hengist and Horsa are the reputed founders of the Kingdom of Kent around AD 450. They continued the peace at first, but chaos ensued when these mercenaries rebelled, leading to fifty years of devastating warfare through the southern counties.*

The gradual cementing of a British nation followed over the next three centuries, before the next assault came, in the early 800s, from the Vikings who would inflict themselves upon the coasts of eastern England for over 200 years. Towards the end, it became simply too much and the scene was set for perhaps the most atrocious event ever to take place in Kent.

GRUESOME TOKENS OF A BLOODBATH

▓ *The darkest of all of our dark days, the gruesome St Brice's Day massacre on 13 November 1002 was perpetrated on tens of thousands of Danes who had settled in the county. The legacy of the day's butchery can still be seen in Kent a thousand years later.*

It was the era of the Viking invasions and much of the southern part of the country was under Viking control. King Ethelred – the Unready – had devised the unheroic response of paying them the Danegeld – in effect, annual protection money to persuade the Danes to behave themselves and not pillage the country any more. It was paid for by a universally unpopular poll tax. For eleven years we continued to stump up sums of up to £24,000 a year to buy peace. (No calculation can give an accurate estimate of what proportion of national wealth this represented – safe to say it was certainly a majority slice.)

The Danegeld ruse had the unexpected (to Ethelred) but not illogical effect of encouraging the Danes to keep pushing up the price of peace. Nor did it completely stop the occasional raid, so by 1002 he had reached the end of his rather long and elastic tether, and conceived what turned out to be a monumental blunder: he gave orders for every Dane in the country to be slaughtered.

Kent had been extremely popular with the Danes as a settling area, mainly because of the proximity to their native shores. The Isle of Sheppey had seen particularly large numbers settle there and consequently it witnessed some of the worst savagery of the whole episode. For centuries afterwards – and even down to the present day for the eagle-eyed – silent testimony to the day's events was given by the vast number of mounds on Sheppey – known locally as 'cotterels', some as high as 20 ft – all over the island: burial places for the thousands killed.

Among the bizarre atrocities of the day was the flaying alive of captured Danes and the subsequent nailing of their skins to the doors of churches, which the Danes were said to have desecrated. Remnants of the skins remained exposed to view at many sites at least into the middle of the 19th century.

Tradition asserts that the gates to Minster Abbey were so decorated for centuries – the Abbey had been a particular target for attack from Danish heathens. The great doors of Rochester Cathedral were also still so adorned well into the 17th century – we have no less an authority than Samuel Pepys' diary, which records a visit he made to the town in April 1661 and his viewing of the Danish skins.

In the long run, it was a blunder of stupendous proportion. One of the victims was the Danish king's sister and the massacre merely prompted ever greater retribution over the next dozen years, which culminated in Ethelred fleeing the throne, leaving the way open for the Danish king's son, Canute, to become king of England in 1016. The Danish conquest was complete.

FEELING IT IN THE BONES

█ *The unfortunate Alphege became Archbishop of Canterbury in June 1006. It should have been the pinnacle of his career but at the time it was a job nobody was very keen to have. For Alphege, the forebodings were fulfilled. He was the first Primate to die a violent death. Only four others have met such a fate, but none as strange as his.*

Alphege had the misfortune to become Primate in the aftermath of the St Brice's Day massacre of 1002. By the time he was installed the Danish revenge was in full flood – and on his doorstep. A large Danish force landed at Sandwich in the summer of 1009 and stormed Canterbury. The complete sack of the city was avoided only by a whip round and the raising of £3,000 (probably in excess of £1 million in today's values) to buy off the attackers.

Not surprisingly the Danes returned for more, a couple of years later. In September 1011 they besieged Canterbury for three weeks until a traitor let them in and this time the city was completely devastated. Some 7,000 are thought to have been slaughtered in the rampage. Alphege was captured and held to ransom. When he refused to appeal to his flock for help in raising the money, his captors found they had on their hands the worst problem a kidnapper could face – a hostage whom no one wanted to bargain for.

Rather confused, they hauled Alphege off and he spent the next seven months being dragged around the county in chains while the Danes decided how to profit from him. By the following Easter they had still not come up with any ideas.

Alphege's curious death was out of frustration more than anything else. On 19 April 1012, the Danish army was at Greenwich. Junior ranks had procured a large supply of wine from their pillaging and they launched into a huge festive feast and binge. Having become uncontrollably drunk they ordered the Archbishop to be brought into the dining hall and demanded instant payment of the ransom. This produced the inevitable negative response, so they began pelting the chained Primate with the remnants of the meal – ox bones. So many struck him that he was bludgeoned to the point of death. He was despatched with a final blow from an axe.

His body was conveyed to St Paul's Cathedral and buried there. A decade later, in an act of repentance, Canute, by then the Danish King of England, had his remains taken back to Canterbury and reburied in the cathedral. The spot in Greenwich where he met his death is marked to this day by a church dedicated in his name.

A MACABRE AND MYSTERIOUS COLLECTION

▉ *The bizarre collection of the bones of up to 4,000 people in the crypt of St Leonard's church in Hythe may be evidence of an ancient murderous massacre in a battle now lost to the historical record.*

The St Leonard's ossuary is one of only two such collections of human bones left in the whole of Britain that are open to the public. It consists of the bones of as many as 4,000 human beings. There are over 2,000 skulls in all, of which 1,200 are neatly stacked a dozen shelves high on both sides of the crypt and over the entrance. Heaped in a huge pile in the middle are the other bones, including, it is estimated, at least 8,000 human thigh bones.

The dimensions of the pile itself are astounding. At the time the first illustrated description was published in 1783, the heap was 30 ft long, 6 ft high and 8 ft wide. A century later it was only 25 ft long, probably due to souvenir hunters.

The origin of the bones is one of Kent's biggest mysteries, and may be evidence of a tremendous, and currently unknown, battle. The first reference to the collection dates from 1678 and this simply tells that they had been deposited in the church before 1600. These uncertainties have allowed local historians a field day for ideas.

The three most frequent explanations contrast the dramatic with the mundane. The dramatic interpretation is that they are the remains of an invading army beaten in a great battle which took place anytime from the 5th to the 13th century. The more prosaic explanations are that they are the accumulated remains of parishioners once buried in the churchyard and regularly removed over the centuries to make

THE ORIGINS OF THE OSSUARY IN ST LEONARD'S, HYTHE, LIE SHROUDED IN MYSTERY.

room for others, or that they are plague victims from the Black Death in the 14th century.

None of the suggestions, however, is conclusive. There are tantalising flaws in each that make a clear-cut answer elusive. The theory of the great battle comes from the investigations made in the late 19th century which, it was maintained, showed that most of the skulls were those of men in the prime of their life (although later investigations in the early 20th century disputed this). The strange white colour of the bones would be consistent with bodies being left out in the open air for a long period before collection. The trouble was that few skulls showed the distinct fractures and incisions that would be likely to result from a savage battle.

If the unusual concentration of male skulls is true, it would tend to rule out theories based on the collection being a cross-section of local population. The cross-section theory has other difficulties. The proponents of this more mundane idea suggest that the bones represent nothing more than regular grave-clearing, However, it is far from clear how so many bones could have been collected from such a small area in so short a time – visitors to the church in the 1540s failed to mention there being a collection at that time. It would be impossible to amass so many bones 'naturally' between then and the first mention of the ossuary some 130 years later. As for the bones being the remains of plague victims, it is argued that it was most unlikely that anyone would think it wise to put the bones of plague victims on display for fear of infection. And no one could suggest the reason for the macabre gathering and displaying of them.

Moreover, the battle-theorists argue back, all the bones appear to be in a similar state of decay. Bones collected over a period would show much more variety in condition. For these theorists, the bones are evidence of a tremendous battle, most likely an invasion from across the Channel, which now, but for these bones, lies lost to the historical record.

Who knows? Perhaps there is an even more down-to-earth explanation. Whatever the truth, the spectacle remains – for those who can stomach it.

THE EXPULSION OF THE JEWS

■ *In 1290, a century of increasing persecution in Britain culminated in an edict from Edward I to expel every Jew in the country, the first example in history of a nation attempting to rid itself entirely of a foreign community.*

By the start of the 13th century, there were 16–20,000 Jews living in Britain in a population of two and a half million. Most had arrived from France since the Norman Conquest a century and a quarter earlier (a large Jewish community had existed in Normandy since Roman times) and there were sizeable Jewish communities in all of England's main cities. They had been subjected to regular bouts of persecution, the most notorious massacre coming at York in 1190 where the whole Jewish community was slaughtered in a night.

On his return from crusading, Edward followed the edict of Pope Gregory X to outlaw money-lending for interest, and the Jews were the natural target. The Statute of Jewry in 1275 banned usury, required all debts to be repaid by the following Easter, and restricted Jews from living outside certain towns and cities. In a foretaste of the persecutions of the Nazi era, this law also required that every Jew over seven years old had to wear a yellow badge on their outer garment measuring at least six inches by three to identify them as Jews.

Their fortunes deteriorating, their freedom of movement hampered, and having few economic outlets allowing them to make their way in the world, increasing evidence (unsurprisingly) emerged of crimes by Jews, particularly coin clipping, which involved shaving off a small portion of the coin, melting down the resultant metal, and selling it on. Hundreds were arrested and thrown into the Tower of London for failure to pay taxes. Some moved successfully into trades – wool in East Anglia and corn in Canterbury – that simply competed with existing local interests and increased tensions further.

Soon a decisive solution was needed. On 18 July 1290, Edward promulgated the edict requiring every professing Jew to leave the realm by 1 November. Any who remained were liable to be executed. They were permitted to take as much of their moveable possessions as they could carry; the non-moveable property was to be forfeited.

Their flight was marked with episodes of great cruelty. Many parties fled through Kent, the quickest route to the Continent, presenting opportunities for highway robbery as they were laden down with their worldly goods. Those who put themselves at the mercy of ships' captains often fared little better. The most infamous incident of all involved a ship sailing from London which had arrived off Queenborough, on the Isle of Sheppey, where the captain anchored at the ebb tide near an exposed sandbank. He invited the passengers to disembark to stretch their legs, and then abandoned them on the sandbank. All drowned as the tide came in.

REVENGE FOR HASTINGS

■ *One hundred and fifty years after the Battle of Hastings, the French marauded through Kent once again – in May 1216 – although this time they were meant to be on the people's side. Prince Louis, eldest son of the French king, was the chosen ally of the English barons in their civil war against King John following the breakdown of the Magna Carta, which had been agreed just a year before. The final defeat of the invaders, at the Battle of Sandwich in the summer of 1217, added a curious first to the annals of warfare.*

Prince Louis had landed at Thanet in mid-May 1216 and, overcoming the last substantial defences of the county at Rochester after just a week's siege, he arrived in London on 2 June. For the next sixteen months Kent was plunged into full scale war the length and breadth of the county. Louis besieged Dover Castle from both the sea and landward side. The royal cause seemed lost when King John died in October, leaving the throne in the hands of his successor, Henry III, who was only nine years old.

Louis decided to spread his troops around and seize the initiative. Lifting the siege of Dover, he allowed the vital breathing space. Thinly spread, he inflicted wide damage throughout the south-east and East Anglia but soon needed reinforcements. He had to fight his way back to Dover to return to France in the spring of 1217 and while he was away the invasion forces crumbled. He could do nothing on his return and a major defeat at Lincoln sent the invaders into free fall. Kent was to be the scene of the bloody endgame.

A last ditch French rescue force was organised at Calais and an 80-ship armada sailed over in August 1217 to try to reach the mouth of the Thames. The Cinque Ports produced 22 ships to defend the coast and the two fleets met in the historic Battle of Sandwich on 24 August. The engagement, in which upwards of 4,000 combatants are said to have perished, unprecedented for a sea battle, warrants mention as it was the first – and possibly only – occurrence in history of the use of chemical warfare at sea.

Although outnumbered four to one, the English fleet had a secret weapon – quicklime. They are said to have loaded the quicklime into pots, which were then shot at the French. With the wind in their favour, the English bursting pots sprayed the enemy, blinding and burning them. They were then butchered with savage brutality, according to the accounts of the battle. The French were pursued almost back to Calais. Louis concluded a quick peace with the young English boy king and within a month left Dover, bound for France. For centuries, the Battle of Sandwich was heralded as the bloody revenge for Hastings. But revenge bred revenge and Sandwich was to be visited again 240 years later.

THE ORIGINS OF A MOURNING TRADITION

Historic retribution for the defeat in the great Battle of Sandwich 240 years earlier was inflicted by a French force of sixty ships that stormed Sandwich and all but demolished the town in August 1457.

Like earlier visitations, the attack was an opportunistic one, taking advantage of another moment in England's history when civil war prevailed. This time it came shortly after the start of the Wars of the Roses. While the dynastic struggle of recent making ensued elsewhere in Britain, the well-nigh prehistoric cross-Channel animosities saw their next round.

Some 1,800 Frenchmen took Sandwich, then very much on the sea's edge, by surprise at about six o'clock on the morning of 28 August by disembarking five miles down the coast and attacking the town from two separate directions. The fighting lasted the entire day. Despite fierce resistance and the urgent calling for reinforcements, which arrived from Hythe and Rye late in the afternoon, the town was utterly devastated.

The Mayor, John Drury, the bailiffs and other officials were captured and summarily executed. Troops ransacked every building and looted jewels, food and any other materials that could be carted back to their ships. A number of wealthy residents were abducted for later ransom and many young women were hauled away with no intention of returning them. By five in the evening the French had retreated, exhausted and replete. They stayed off the coast until October, provoking a constant fear of repetition.

The massacre of the town's civic leaders was wholesale and caused particular outrage. In a tradition that is still kept to this day, every mayor of Sandwich wears a black robe and has carried before him a black wand as a sign of permanent mourning. It is said that it took the town a hundred years to recover from the day's events. On the 500th anniversary of the attack, the mayor of Sandwich visited Honfleur in Normandy, the harbour from where the invasion was launched. The two towns are now twinned.

The immediate sequel to these events for Sandwich was highly ironic. In the turmoil of civil war, a desperately practical decision was made by the king to retrieve the situation in the Channel. In the national interest, Henry VI appointed his arch enemy Richard, Earl of Warwick ('The Kingmaker'), the legendary baron, as 'Keeper of the Sea'. Warwick quickly chased the French away and seized Calais. He then returned to his older loyalties, gathered a force against the king and in January 1460 re-invaded England – where else, but at Sandwich.

The town now had the dubious distinction of having been assailed by the English as well as the French. It must have been a happy day indeed for the burghers of the town when the sea eventually retreated far enough for Sandwich to no longer be a port.

THE LAST INVASION OF ENGLAND

█ *The last seizure of English soil by a foreign invader occurred in June 1667 during one of the English Navy's most humiliating defeats in its history. All the action took place on our doorstep, on the river Medway, as a huge Dutch flotilla bombarded Chatham, the principal British naval base of the day.*

England had been at war with the Dutch since 1664, the second conflict between the two countries in a dozen years. Theirs were the two greatest navies of the age and the struggle was for nothing less than supremacy over the trading routes throughout the world. A number of actions over the previous two years in the North Sea and the English Channel had been indecisive and peace talks were under way. The Dutch, however, had taken advantage of the outbreak of plague in London and the Great Fire the year after, to assume control of the Thames and for most of this year, 1667, had been able to cruise unmolested in British waters.

With peace talks threatening, the commander of the Dutch fleet, Admiral de Ruyter, decided on one last effort to improve the Dutch position at the negotiating table – in modem parlance, he went in search of a few bargaining chips. Bizarrely, the English ship carrying the mediators to Holland to conduct the talks passed de Ruyter's fleet as it prepared to leave Dutch waters and was saluted by the Dutch flagship.

The Dutch armada of 72 ships, 13,000 sailors and 3,000 soldiers moored menacingly in the Thames estuary and over the weekend of 8–9 June ships patrolled up and down the river causing panic ashore. The first attack – and the landing of Dutch troops – came at 5 pm on 10 June. It took just a 90-minute bombardment of the new fort at Sheerness for it to be abandoned and 800 Dutch soldiers came ashore and took control (led, oddly, by an English mercenary, one Colonel Dolman).

They ransacked the fort and carried off its stores and supplies of food. The next day they demolished the sea wall, flooding the fort and surrounding land, and made their way inland to Queenborough, which fell without a fight. The mayor, having decided to spare needless bloodshed and destruction, according to some accounts hoisted a white flag from the town hall – the only civic centre in England since the Norman Conquest ever to have flown the flag of surrender to a foreign enemy. For a while it also had a foreign flag flying over it, another unique but dubious honour.

Sheppey remained in possession of the Dutch for 11 days – days which were put to acquisitive use by a comprehensive but apparently civilly conducted programme of looting, in which thousands of head of sheep and cattle, food and other supplies were carted off to the Dutch ships.

The occupation of Sheppey was, however, a sideshow to the main attack, which came on 12 June when the Dutch fleet attacked Chatham, the first time a hostile fleet had sailed up the Medway since the Vikings nearly nine centuries before. It was a patently unequal battle. The English Navy lost half its ships, including the three largest ships it possessed. The most galling loss was the Dutch capture of the flagship of the Navy, the *Royal Charles*, which was towed away as booty.

On the same day, the Dutch also landed troops in Gillingham – the second occupation of English soil. Contemporary accounts say that the townsfolk of Gillingham found no cause to complain about the soldiers' behaviour. It seems they were considered to have behaved better in fact than the English soldiers who had been quartered until recently in the village.

The battles lasted for the rest of the week until the Dutch retired to consolidate for a second assault. The initiative swung to the English and slowly the Dutch were beaten off. By the end of the month they were a spent force, but had achieved their aim. Within weeks the peace treaty was signed, on much more favourable terms for the Dutch than they had expected.

JUNE 1667: *THE DUTCH IN THE MEDWAY* BY VAN SOEST PORTRAYS THE ATTACK ON CHATHAM AND THE CAPTURE OF THE NAVY'S FLAGSHIP *ROYAL CHARLES* (CENTRE) AS A WAR PRIZE.

WAR AND BATTLE – MODERN TIMES

BRITAIN'S FIRST AIR RAID

■ *The first successful air raid on British soil took place shortly before 11 o'clock in the morning on Christmas Eve 1914. The war was five months old.*

THE RECIPIENT OF THIS DUBIOUS DISTINCTION was Dover, and to be precise one Mr T. A. Terson residing at the end of Leyburne Road, 400 yards from the castle, the presumed target.

The first ever hostile bomb on Britain dropped into his back garden and exploded, shattering several windows in the vicinity and leaving a hole 10 ft wide and 4 ft deep in his cabbage patch. *The Times* later reported picturesquely that 'small pieces of cabbage were scattered some distance on all sides'. There was just one human casualty, a gardener named Banks who was working in the nearby grounds of St James' rectory. He was cutting holly, ivy and other evergreens for the church Christmas decorations and was up a tree at the time. Despite being blown out of it and falling to the ground, he was not seriously hurt. The aircraft responsible made only this single attack and immediately turned round and headed back across the Channel.

Curious though the incident was, the reason for the raid was even more bizarre. There was no military objective in the exercise. It came as the result of the antics of the First World War equivalent of our modern day tabloid press.

A newspaper in Germany had offered a prize for the first German airman to drop a bomb on Britain. The successful pilot of the mission, a Lieutenant von Prondynski, became a fleeting hero in Germany and got the Iron Cross for his efforts. He was thought to have stayed in Dover on a visit earlier in the year before the war began and knew clearly what he was aiming for. He missed the castle – the likely target – by just a few yards.

There was a mad scramble for souvenirs from the raid. Fragments of the bomb were mounted on a shield and presented to the king at Buckingham Palace and other remnants were auctioned as paperweights in aid of charity. True to human nature, there turned out to be far more bits eventually sold by opportunists than probably ever landed that morning. Everyone seemed to have miraculously found a piece or knew someone who had one to sell.

It had in fact been the second attempted air raid that week. The first ended harmlessly on 20 December as a couple of bombs fell into the sea without reaching land. During the First World War – the first conflict where aircraft came of age as weapons – Dover suffered almost two hundred bombings by aircraft, not to mention the raids by the *Gotha* airships.

Curiously, as well as being the first town ever hit in Britain, Dover was also the last to be bombed in the First World War. In the early hours of 20 May 1918, four bombs fell around Priory station, another six at St Margaret's and the last one, about 1 am, on Swingate Aerodrome.

THE GERMAN INVASION TUNNEL SCARE

The failure of Hitler's plans for an invasion of Britain in 1940 did not prevent some outlandish fears to grow about the vulnerability of the country, and especially Kent, to the threat of German attack. Perhaps the strangest was the fear that the Germans were plotting to tunnel their way across the Channel.

The scare was not finally laid to rest until November 1942 when the Allied invasion of North Africa turned the war's tide and put the Axis powers on the defensive for the rest of the conflict. It was only then that the home authorities felt able to completely discount the possibility of a German invasion of Britain.

Far-fetched though an invasion tunnel scheme may sound, the wartime atmosphere allowed even the most fanciful ideas to gain ground and official consideration.

Ironically, it had been the sudden cancellation of the surface invasion in the late summer of 1940 after the Battle of Britain that started to fuel rumours of a more devilishly cunning scheme. Through breaking German codes early on in the war, British military intelligence knew on the day Hitler postponed the invasion, 17 September, that the imminent threat was over, but this only started some senior scientists in the corridors of Whitehall worrying seriously about a subterranean threat.

The German Channel tunnel was to become one of the war's great red herrings, for a while exercising some of the highest minds in the land. The change in the fortunes of the war by late 1942 was significant because the timescale the Germans were thought to be working to was in the order of twelve years. A tunnel was only a threat if the war developed into one of Napoleonic length. From now on, it was clear it would not. It brought an end to two frustrating years in which imaginations ran riot without one solid shred of evidence ever emerging that a tunnel was actually being dug.

It is now known that no such plans ever indeed existed. The circumstantial evidence at the time, however, seemed ominous. In late 1940 and early 1941, suspicions grew in Whitehall about the sudden German abandonment of the invasion (Hitler had in fact decided to concentrate on the invasion of Russia).

The government scientific advisory committee discussed a document sent to it by one engineer who warned that the Germans could be planning not just a single tunnel but one which fanned out to 15 or 20 exit tunnels under the Kent countryside from which vertical lift shafts would be dug to within 20 feet of the surface. At the appropriate time, with tanks in place below waiting to be raised on mechanical lifts, the tops of the shafts would be blasted away and the tanks would roll out over Kent. That such a bizarre conception received close attention within government circles indicates the underlying fear that pervaded Britain at the time that just about anything was possible.

In November 1941 an eminent scientist, Sir Henry Dale, a high-ranking member of the scientific committee as well as being President of the Royal Society, produced another paper warning that the threat should be investigated closely and that a tunnel could in fact be built in as little as 20 months. He warned that one of the ways the Germans could speed up work would be to dispose of the waste produced by the tunnelling by crushing it up and dissolving it into slurry which could be pumped into the Channel.

So seriously was the idea taken that, in the spring of 1942, the Admiralty were asked, and agreed, to order all ships in the Channel to keep watch on the colour of the water to spot telltale traces of dissolved chalk.

But the strangest plans were established on shore along the coast around Dover. R. A. Butler, who later achieved high government office, was then Chairman of the Science Committee and he recommended an elaborate listening experiment to be carried out to detect the sound of Germans chipping away below ground. A high-powered delegation of scientists visited the coast in July 1942. They first thought about reactivating the abandoned 1880 and 1920 tunnel workings at Shakespeare Cliff to test their microphones but this proved impractical. So they recommended that a party of Royal Engineers be sent into the tunnels within Dover cliffs with pick-axes to make tunnelling noises.

Such experiments, bizarre though they may seem now, were actually conducted in September 1942. It was found that it was possible to hear 'small noises' – single pick-axes – at a distance of around 200 yards and 'large noises' – mechanical borers – at something up to a mile. The report on the experiments recommended the setting up of a chain of fifty listening posts strung out along the 10 miles of coast considered most vulnerable.

That was as far as the scheme got. It went for approval before the Science Committee in the autumn of 1942 as preparations for the invasion of North Africa were being finalised. With Allied success, the invasion scare receded, the listening posts were never built and one of the war's strangest sideshows came to an end.

THE TRAIN THAT SHOT DOWN A PLANE

■ *One of the Second World War's oddest deaths was that of an unidentified German airman who was hit by a British train – while he was still piloting his aircraft. The train that shot down a plane ranks as one of the strangest episodes of the war in Kent.*

It happened in November 1942, in mid-afternoon over Ashford. A pair of German fighter planes on a scavenging mission spotted the 3.18 pm Lydd to Ashford train, which had just started out on its journey packed with troops going on leave. Both planes dived and attacked, the first raking the steam engine with machine-gun fire causing the boiler to explode, sending debris up high into the air. The dome behind the funnel was propelled sharply upwards smashing into the underside of the second attacking plane, which was now directly overhead. The plane careered out of control, hit a telegraph wire and crashed into the field alongside the track. The pilot did not survive and his companion headed off to safety across the Channel.

The strangest victim of the war in Kent was buried for the duration of the conflict in Lydd cemetery. Afterwards, in common with all the others, his body was exhumed and reburied in the national German war cemetery in Staffordshire.

KENT ON THE FRONT LINE AGAIN

■ *A week after D-Day and just when the home front might have good reason to think it had had its last taste of battle, Kent became the first to experience a new era of warfare. The county became the most frequent site for a landing of the deadly doodlebug.*

The first of a new breed of terror weapon winged its way across the Channel in the general direction of London in the early morning of 13 June 1944. It was the first attack by V1 flying bombs, and at 4.18 am the first came down on British soil – a piece of waste ground at Swanscombe. A second fell, two minutes later, at Cuckfield next door in Sussex, killing several farm animals. Two more came in that first wave – the third at 5.07 am at Crouch near Sevenoaks and the last, the only one to reach the capital and the only one to inflict human injuries, landed on a railway bridge at Bethnal Green killing six and wounding nine. They were the only successes in a battery of 27 flying bombs sent over that morning. All the rest failed to arrive over Britain, either going off course even before leaving France or, in the majority of cases, falling short into the Channel.

The weapons were designed with terror rather than destruction in mind. Although the rockets' fuel supplies were crudely calibrated to exhaust over London, their high degree of unreliability made it a lottery for victims. They heralded a new style of warfare, different from the blitz that Britain had endured since 1940.

Previous air raids were intense and usually at night, offering a respite in between. The flying bomb ushered in a period of continuous raiding with the missiles launched day and night. Upwards of 100 a day were arriving at the peak. They added a psychological edge too. They were slow, visible and very audible. To observe one on its course induced a sense of inevitability about its path and powerlessness to do much about it. The notoriously awful silence that came with the cutting out of the engine when its fuel ran out increased the tension further for the last few moments before impact.

The country was only told of the new weapon three days later after a second mass attack on the night of 14/15 June which saw 50 land on London, causing severe fires throughout the capital, although still only one in five launches were successful – the raid had unleashed 244 rockets.

At first the government announced that they were radio-controlled devices, implying some rudiments of logic to the targets hit. Whether this was a genuine belief or whether it was an attempt to conceal the arbitrary nature of the threat in order to calm fraying nerves will probably never be known. It lasted just a week. By the 19th speculation about the unguided missiles in the newspapers had been confirmed. They quickly acquired their nicknames, first 'buzz-bomb' because of the throbbing sound of the engine, and then, more curiously, the 'doodlebug'.

Kent was the alleyway for the V1s heading towards London. Not surprisingly, the county bore most of the brunt of the often wayward and unpredictable weapon. The authorities quickly responded by putting in place a heavy concentration of 2,500 anti-aircraft guns in the county and set up a dramatic 1,600-strong balloon barrage covering an arc along the face of the North Downs. This would bring down many missiles before they reached London – but onto the rural peace of Kent villages.

In the three-month campaign before the launch sites in France were seized, some 8,600 of the weapons were launched on Britain. Only two-thirds ever reached the mainland and fewer than half of those actually made it through the defensive lines to land in the capital. Of the 2,636 that landed, 1,672 came down in Kent. They caused 750 deaths (far less a toll than the over 5,000 who died from those hitting London) and nearly 10,000 injuries.

In July, flying bomb attacks were reported on every day of the month and on every day bar one in August. On 3 August, 101 doodlebugs were shot down in a single day.

Although not suffering the magnitude of catastrophe that occurred in London – the worst V1 incident killed 119 people and injured 141 at the Wellington Barracks near Buckingham Palace on 20 June – Kent had its own tragic stories. On 30 June, a V1 hit Weald House at Crockham Hill, which was being used as a child evacuation centre; 22 of the 30 children and 8 of the 11 adults were killed. All the children were under five. In Beckenham a restaurant was hit during lunchtime and it took three days to excavate the victims. Of the 67 casualties, 44 were deaths. When a V1 landed near a bus queue in Penge, 15 died and 107 were injured. The official history gruesomely added that 'considerable difficulty was found in identifying the victims'.

After September, when the French bases were overrun, attacks eased off significantly, to less than one a day. To the war's end, only another 45 hit Kent, along with nearly 150 of the next generation V2 rockets.

Despite all the horrors, it could have been even worse. A bizarre footnote emerged after the war. The Germans were well aware of the inaccuracy of the weapons, which were at the cutting edge of technology. As the plans for the opening of the V1 attack were being laid, Hitler received a startling request from Germany's leading woman aviator, the celebrated Hanna Reitsch. She asked for a personal meeting with the Führer and told him that the V1 was too inaccurate. A piloted rocket was the answer and she offered herself as the first volunteer. The concept of kamikaze rockets reached production stage with 175 piloted versions of the V1 ready for use by October 1944 and 90 pilots trained. But they were never used. Hanna Reitsch made her contribution to the programme by flying a V1 on over 20 successful test flights. Why Hitler decided against the concept is one of the remaining mysteries of the war.

A FOOTNOTE TO THE TALE OF MODERN WEAPONS

Alongside the beginning of this new era of warfare ran a more familiar vein. Kent had been the only part of the British Isles vulnerable from as early as the First World War to shellfire emanating from across the Channel. An official tally compiled shortly after the Second World War documented over 3,500 occasions of shells landing on Kent from artillery fired from the Continent: 85 per cent struck Dover and its surroundings, but other coastal towns also suffered – Folkestone had 218 hits, Deal 127 and Ramsgate 56. The intensity grew during the V1 blitz in 1944. On 26 September 50 shells landed on Dover. Bizarrely, in a German attempt to mask the very first doodlebug raid on 13 June, Maidstone gained the dubious distinction of being the furthest English town ever to be hit by a shell fired from France, over sixty miles away.

3

ACCIDENTS

YOUNG LIVES WIPED OUT IN KENT'S WORST ROAD ACCIDENT

■ *At the time, the Dock Road disaster on 4 December 1951 was the worst road accident to have occurred in Britain and remained so until 1975. It happened shortly before six o'clock on a murky night near the front gates of Chatham naval dockyard.*

A CONTINGENT OF ROYAL MARINE CADETS – fifty-two of them – aged between 8 and 15, were marching on the side of the road down the notoriously long and sweeping hill that connects Brompton to Chatham. A double-decker bus, approaching from behind, ploughed into them, killing twenty-four and injuring nineteen. Only the nine at the very front avoided injury completely. Seventeen boys were killed outright at the scene.

The boys had been on their way to a boxing tournament at the main dockyard and had been marching in double file from Melville Barracks in Brompton. All the elements of tragedy conspired on that evening to bring about catastrophe. The boys were marching on the left-hand side of the road – in the direction of traffic – so they never saw the bus approach them. The bus driver later confirmed that he did not have his headlights on, only sidelights. The road was notoriously poorly lit, with visibility further hampered by the high brick wall that ran down one side of the road.

The driver never even saw what he had hit. He told the inquest later that he was travelling at normal speed when he suddenly felt a series of bumps 'as if the bus had run over a lot of loose stones'.

Hundreds of car owners in the Medway towns volunteered their vehicles to ferry parents of the casualties to the three hospitals handling the disaster. The national press reported the following day that the bus driver, who had been with the company for forty years, had been due to attend a ceremony at Maidstone the day after the accident to receive a medal for 25 years' safe driving. The report turned out to be untrue but for a short time added cruel irony to the unfolding story.

WOODLANDS CEMETERY, GILLINGHAM, 12 DECEMBER, 1951: THE FUNERAL CORTEGE OF 20 OF THE 24 YOUNG NAVAL CADETS WHO DIED IN THE DOCK ROAD DISASTER. (COURTESY OF MEDWAY COUNCIL: LOCAL STUDIES COLLECTION)

THEY MARCHED AND DIED TOGETHER AND WERE LAID TO REST TOGETHER.
(COURTESY OF MEDWAY COUNCIL: LOCAL STUDIES COLLECTION)

Further fateful twists emerged at the inquest ten days later. The commanding officer told how, shortly before the accident, he had ordered two boys near the front to go to the back of the pack because they were marching out of step. That small transgression cost them their lives as they were the first to be hit. Despite question marks over the bus driving, the jury took an hour and twenty minutes to return a verdict of accidental death.

On 12 December, a mass funeral was held for twenty of the victims. A service took place in Rochester Cathedral with the twenty coffins draped with the union flag and wreaths laid out together. Thousands stood outside to hear the service relayed by loudspeaker. Thousands more, five and six deep, lined the road to Woodlands cemetery, Gillingham. The procession of coffins was a mile long.

At the cemetery on each of the graves was placed a posy of violets sent anonymously, inscribed 'In memory of the very gallant little lads who kept in step to the end'. Throughout the evening, the muffled bells of the cathedral tolled.

Despite the inquest verdict of accidental death, public pressure mounted for the bus driver to be prosecuted. The authorities succumbed and his case was hastily transferred to the Old Bailey and was heard just six weeks later. Although the jury found him guilty it recommended maximum leniency. The judge fined him £20 and disqualified him for three years, saying that no punishment the court could award could compare with that which he must have undergone already.

THE THAMES' WORST CATASTROPHE

■ *Britain's worst civilian shipping disaster occurred in the Thames at Gallions Reach, Woolwich, in the early evening of 3 September 1878 when the* Princess Alice, *a pleasure steamer packed with day-trippers, was rammed by a cargo ship. Almost eight hundred people drowned.*

The disaster happened as the paddle steamer was returning to the centre of the capital after one of its regular day trips down river to Sheerness. These jaunts were immensely popular with poorer

Londoners who were rarely able to escape the city. On this day, an unusually warm one for late summer, the ship had been packed to the gunwales. No agreed passenger figure would ever be produced. The ship was licensed to carry up to 900, but witness evidence suggested she may have been substantially overloaded that evening.

As she made her way back up river, the *Princess Alice* had called at Gravesend just after six o'clock and was approaching her next stop at North Woolwich pier. With dusk falling, at just after 7.30 pm she encountered in the lowering gloom the steamer *Bywell Castle* coming down from London. The later inquiry into the disaster blamed the lack of standard rules for passing as the cause of the collision. As *The*

DISASTER ON THE THAMES: THE *PRINCESS ALICE* IS RAMMED
WITH THE LOSS OF UP TO 800 LIVES.

Times quaintly put it, the catastrophe stemmed from the two vessels 'in the moment of peril, each taking the wrong course to avoid each other's blunder, and, like the meeting of two embarrassed pedestrians on the footpath, rushing into each other's bosoms'.

The *Bywell Castle* slammed into the smaller *Princess Alice* amidships, cutting her in two, and breaking pipes which sent scalding steam showering over the panicking passengers. The collision took place a mere 300 yards offshore, but few survived. Weighed down with the heavy clothes of the day, most had no chance of rescue. The *Princess Alice* sank in just four minutes.

No one will ever know the true number of victims. Accounts vary from 550 (the toll recorded on the memorial to the disaster which stands today in Woolwich cemetery) to up to 786 given by the authoritative *Guinness Book of Records*.

There were some poignant stories amidst the tragedy. The superintendent of the London Steamboat Company, the owners of the *Princess Alice*, took control of managing the rescue operation despite having lost his wife and four of his children in the accident. A Kilburn woman, returning from a stay in Sheerness, had decided to travel separately from her husband and cousin who were going by train because of her fears about rail safety following a train crash at Sittingbourne three days earlier. She took the 'safe' river route instead, and drowned.

As civilian accidents go, nothing approaching the scale of the disaster has ever been seen in Britain, before or since. Unparalleled too were the grisly stories which followed as bodies were washed up all along the river from Limehouse to Erith for days afterwards. Looters rifled through corpses, hacking off fingers and hands to steal jewellery. Boatmen, who were being paid by the authorities five shillings for every body recovered, fought over torsos as they were discovered. Some bodies were even stolen from the makeshift mortuary and re-sold back for another bounty.

Near the site of the memorial at Woolwich, some 120 of the victims were buried in a mass grave, including the captain of the *Princess Alice* who died with his ship and most of his family who were also on board at the time.

A HOLIDAY FIRE TRAGEDY

■ *On 11 July 1929, Gillingham was the scene of a tragic and bizarre fire disaster that shocked all of Britain. It happened during the town's fête, a fund-raising event for the local hospital, held annually in Gillingham Park.*

The fête was Gillingham's event of the year. The two days of festivities traditionally culminated in a spectacular display by the local fire brigade. Every year, they staged a realistic rescue of a number of people supposedly trapped in a specially-built, three-storey, wooden and canvas 'house' nearly 40 ft tall, after which the whole contraption was set alight for real to be doused by the fire engines.

It all made for an exciting finale and had been a regular feature of the fête for the past twenty years. Every year, hundreds of local children vied to take part in the charade. On this occasion, nine boys, naval cadets and sea scouts aged between 10 and 14, joined six firemen dressed in fancy costumes, pretending to be a wedding party. They paraded shortly before ten o'clock as dusk began to gather and the spectacle commenced. Proud families watched from the crowd as their bright, young and excited children got into the act.

The plan involved lighting a small fire on the first floor to produce realistic smoke effects. For reasons unknown – possibly, it is thought, a dignitary mistakenly lighting the wrong part – the real bonfire at the bottom was ignited.

The thousands of spectators watched totally oblivious to the real disaster unfolding before them and as the smoke billowed up they continued to cheer and applaud this year's display as being more realistic than ever. The screaming from the occupants sounded more lifelike than it had ever done and the bodies burning inside the building looked so real. Only when two boys leapt from the top of the structure to their deaths on the ground below did the crowd start to realise that a major tragedy was occurring.

As the firemen tackled the blaze, aware from an early stage that matters had gone drastically wrong, the exterior of the house disintegrated, leaving just a grim skeleton of charred beams. All

THIS PICTURE IS BELIEVED TO SHOW THE EARLY CONSTRUCTION OF THE MOCK HOUSE IN THE DAYS BEFORE THE 'FIREMAN'S WEDDING' BONFIRE. (COURTESY OF MEDWAY ARCHIVES AND KENT FIRE & RESCUE SERVICE MUSEUM)

THE FUNERAL PROCESSION THROUGH GILLINGHAM FOR THE VICTIMS OF THE 'FIREMAN'S WEDDING' DISASTER. (COURTESY OF MEDWAY ARCHIVES AND KENT FIRE & RESCUE SERVICE MUSEUM)

fifteen people in the holocaust died. One fireman was seen to jump from the top with a boy under each arm in a desperate effort to escape, to no avail. One account described the most sickening image of the tragedy as being the sight of the frail burning body of a boy half dangling over the edge of the upper floor, ever so slowly slipping back from view into the flames.

As in so many tragedies, sad vignettes emerged. One boy had only been asked the night before to take part. He would not have been there otherwise. Two others, inseparable friends, were soon to have been split up as one was to move to London. They were dreading the parting. In the words of one account, 'The charred remains of their little bodies were found together in the mound of ashes at the foot of the burnt-out house. Death had spared them the separation that life had planned to thrust upon them.'

That so many died in so public a fashion – at least three mothers saw their boys perish in the fire – touched the whole nation. The king and queen sent a telegram of sympathy and a mass funeral was held six days later for which thousands lined the route through Gillingham. A mile-and-a-half-long procession of fire appliances carried the fifteen coffins from St Augustine's church to Woodlands cemetery where they were buried in a communal grave. It was said that never in its long history had Gillingham known an occasion so touching and overwhelming. (Sadly, it would exceed that solemnity a generation later in the funeral for the Dock Road disaster, also involving young cadets.)

At the inquest there were conflicting accounts about where the fire started and at the end no one was any the wiser as to how the tragedy had occurred. A verdict of misadventure was returned.

A DICKENS OF A SCRAPE

■ *The day that Kent almost killed Charles Dickens: 9 June 1865.*

In the middle of the afternoon, just before reaching the village of Staplehurst, south of Maidstone, the Folkestone to London boat train careered round a bend onto a little stone bridge and derailed itself in one of Kent's earliest train disasters. Six of the seven passenger coaches crashed from the bridge into the stream 15 ft below. Ten people died and fifty-two were injured.

More remarkable was the fact that just one coach survived intact, hanging precariously over the edge of the bridge, leaving its occupants shocked but unhurt. There were just three, and one of them was Charles Dickens. By his own account, which he wrote still in a state of shock the following day, he tended to some of the injured as best he could and saw at least two people die of their injuries in front of his eyes.

It was an incident which remained with him for the rest of his life and he frequently recounted the events with undisguised horror. He wrote more than three years later that 'my escape in the Staplehurst accident ... is not to be obliterated from my nervous system. To this hour I have sudden vague rushes of terror ... which are perfectly unreasonable but quite insurmountable.'

He was never the same person after the mishap. He was unable to sit in a horse carriage in crowded streets without feeling petrified and doubted that he could actually ride a horse at speed himself ever again. He constantly remarked to friends how the accident had wrecked his nerves and how he suffered recurring nightmares in

The Staplehurst rail crash which nearly killed Charles Dickens. In fact, only one carriage, not three pictured here, remained on the track.

which he 'lived it all over again'. Coincidentally – or perhaps as a result of the real fear it continued to provoke in him – he died on the anniversary of the crash five years later.

The accident had been caused by a curious, and avoidable, oversight. Railway workers were repairing the track at the time on that Friday afternoon and had removed a section of it on the bridge for replacement. The foreman in charge had, as always, the weekly timetable from the railway company giving him the times of the boat trains whose journeys varied depending on the tides, which governed ferry sailings.

The enquiry into the disaster found that the timetable showed the correct time for the arrival of the train in the area to be 3.15 pm, but for some reason that was never explained the foreman believed the train was not due until 5.20 pm. He had not bothered to consult the timetable book that day. This reluctance to read a book ironically almost caused the death of one of the English language's greatest exponents.

The physical distress caused to Dickens that day and for the rest of his life was only part of the discomfort the crash created. Publicity surrounding the accident and its eminent victim was quick to circulate and was most unwelcome to Dickens since he had been travelling in the carriage with two women, one being 26-year-old Nelly Ternan, a celebrated actress of the day with whom he had been maintaining a liaison for over eight years (Dickens was now 53). He, Nelly and her mother were coming back to Britain from France where they had spent a discreet holiday. Being discovered in such company (although authorities disagree about whether he had a full blown affair, and possibly a child who died in infancy) did not do his reputation any favours at all.

A WARTIME CATASTROPHE

■ *On 2 April 1916, at the height of the First World War, the Sunday lunchtime peace of Uplees Marsh near Faversham was shattered by what was the worst accident of its kind ever in Britain. Only a similar munitions accident two years later, in Nottingham, has been more deadly.*

This out-of-the-way area of the county, the shoreline of the Thames, had since the 16th century been crowded with gunpowder and dynamite factories. By the turn of the 20th century it was the centre of Britain's explosives industry. Thousands of workers clustered in the manufacturing sheds, working flat out for the war effort.

Shortly after noon, a small fire started among empty linen sacks at the Explosives Loading Company. Although it was noticed, no one apparently tried to put it out, concentrating instead on moving stocks of the highly flammable TNT away from the area. A large crowd of curious workers on their lunch break gathered to see what the fuss was about.

At 1.20 pm they found out. The whole place went up, setting off an equally terrifying explosion at the Cotton Powder Company, which made nitroglycerine, next door. Just 20 minutes later, a third explosion destroyed a factory half a mile down the road, which made primers for mines and whose roof had been set alight by the initial blast.

In all, 106 people died and 100 more were injured. The blasts were so destructive that there was no trace left of five buildings which had been there just two hours before. An account by a local doctor who attended the scene recorded that five National Guardsmen who were closest to the explosion were all killed instantly. 'Of one, nothing but his rifle was ever found.'

The explosion broke windows for 20 miles around, was heard over 50 miles away, and rattled windows as far away as Norwich and Great Yarmouth. It inflicted extensive damage in Southend across the river and it caused the cross to topple from the altar in St Peter's church in Shoeburyness 15 miles away across the estuary.

Little more is known about what exactly happened that day and how so many came to lose their lives. Wartime reporting restrictions prevented information from emerging. One discovery after the event was ironic. At the site of the initial explosion, the company had been preparing a water supply system for fire control. The connection to the water mains had been laid on and hydrants were ready for installation, but due to a delivery error the pumps required to complete the system had been left off the consignment. This oversight possibly allowed the original fire to burn longer than it might have. To fight the fire when it broke out, a chain of men had to pass buckets of water up from the dyke hundreds of yards away.

An official inquiry, conducted in secret, reached the conclusion that the casualties were so high because so many had gathered in the confined area. The inspector alluded to the rumour among survivors that most of the dead were casual – wartime draftees – unfamiliar with and unappreciative of the danger that was unfolding. It seems that the old factory hands had mostly left in a hurry, fully aware of the impending catastrophe.

A mass funeral was held four days later at the poignantly-named Love Lane cemetery in Faversham where the awesome 100-ft-long grave still lies today, looking like a raised lawn bounded by a granite wall and surmounted by a 12-ft granite cross. The inscription to those interred there says simply that they died in the service of their country. There is nothing to signify that it is anything other than just another war memorial.

The site of the explosion itself has now returned to being open grassland, an appropriately empty legacy to that quiet Sunday afternoon which disintegrated so suddenly and completely.

WHEN THE NAVY HAD TO SINK ITS OWN SHIP

■ *Dover saw its most tragic and bizarre marine accident on 16 September 1918 when the Royal Navy deliberately sank one of its own ships – just five days after it had entered into service.*

The fleet had gathered in the harbour in readiness, if needed, for an invasion of the Continent as the last battles of the First World War were being fought. Among them were two ships that should not have been there at all. Oddly named the *Bjoergvin* and the *Nidaros*, they had been ordered by the Norwegian government before the war but had, on their completion, been commandeered by the Royal Navy for the allied war effort. They had been finished during the summer and had just sailed down the North Sea from their shipyard on Tyneside after completing their sea trials. Formally commissioned into the Royal Navy the week before, they now moored under their new

HMS *GLATTON* LAY EXPOSED AT LOW TIDE FOR EIGHT YEARS IN DOVER HARBOUR BEFORE BEING SALVAGED.

names, HMS *Gorgon* and HMS *Glatton*, stocked up with ammunition and battle-ready as coastal bombardment ships.

It was the *Glatton* that figured in the tragedy. Shortly after six o'clock in the evening, without warning, she blew up in a gigantic explosion that shattered every window for miles around. Fortunately a munitions ship moored nearby was able to slip away or the disaster would have been even greater. As the *Glatton* was engulfed in flames and with screams for help coming from below decks, the Admiral of the Port gave the order to sink her with torpedoes as the only way to extinguish the fire and avoid risking further explosions from ammunition stored in the ship.

It took four torpedoes to do the job from fellow destroyers *Cossack* and *Myngs*. From the keeled-over hulk of the *Glatton*, 60 bodies were recovered and over 120 sailors were injured, of whom 19 later died. *Glatton* had lost nearly two-thirds of her crew, all agonisingly sacrificed by their commander to prevent even worse carnage.

The inquiry that later investigated the accident established that the explosion was caused by cork lagging catching fire from hot ashes being placed next to the bulkhead in the adjacent boiler room. Unbelievably, no one had told the engine room that the hold next to it was an ammunition store.

An even more bizarre theory came to light only many years later when the *Glatton*'s sister ship *Gorgon* underwent a refit. Large areas of the ship which should have been packed with heat resistant cork were found in fact to be empty or stuffed with editions of the *Newcastle Evening Chronicle*. Hundreds of rivets were also missing, giving rise to speculation that a similar condition might have prevailed on the *Glatton* and that the heat from the engine room had passed through the rivet holes and ignited the paper wadding in between. In the end, it looked as if it was most likely to have been lazy workmanship that laid the seeds of the tragedy.

The *Glatton* – the ship that lasted less than a week and never fought in anger – lay on the harbour floor for eight years, exposed at each low tide. In March 1926, she was finally salvaged, cut up and the pieces were buried beneath reclaimed land now used by the car ferry terminal at Dover's Eastern Dock.

THE LOSS OF THE *TRUCULENT*

A catalogue of errors and bad luck in January 1950 led to what at the time was the Royal Navy's worst post-war disaster when one of its most modern submarines sank in the Thames estuary. Catastrophically, it later emerged that nearly all the crew had in fact managed to escape from the stricken craft but had succumbed to the cold or been swept away by strong tides. What had apparently been a textbook evacuation had actually served to create a tragedy.

The submarine HMS *Truculent*, seven years old and a veteran of the Pacific War, had been at Chatham for a refit and was undergoing diving trials in the North Sea. She was carrying 79 men, including 18 civilian dock workers. Having completed her trials on 12 January, she was returning that evening, on the surface, to her temporary base at Sheerness.

THE *TRUCULENT* BEING RAISED, TWO MONTHS AFTER HER SINKING.

Also out that night, heading towards the sea, was a small Swedish cargo vessel, the *Divina*, bound for Ipswich. She was carrying a consignment of paraffin and, believing she was following regulations, she mounted an additional red warning light on top of her mast to signify she had a dangerous cargo. Ironically, it was this over-concern for safety that was to lead to the catastrophe that unfolded.

The next in the sequence of misjudgments came when the *Truculent*'s escort ship decided she no longer needed to accompany her and steamed on ahead towards her base further along the river at Chatham. That decision too was to be a significant factor in the disaster.

Around 7 pm, eight miles out from Sheerness in the middle of the estuary off Whitstable, the lookout on the *Truculent* spotted the unusual array of lights in the gloom. In particular the extra red light bemused the crew. Both the Officer of the Watch and then the Captain were summoned to the conning tower, but even after calling for their seamanship manual, neither could distinguish clearly what the light signalled. The extra red light was entirely unfamiliar to them. They concluded that it indicated a stationary ship moored in the river. As the waters to the north were shallow, the Captain felt he could not pass her to the starboard side as the normal rules required, so he ordered the *Truculent* to turn towards the middle of the river.

The vessel had barely started on its fatal manoeuvre before it became clear that the lights were not only not stationary, but were also much closer than thought. The *Divina* rammed the starboard side of the submarine. The Captain of the *Truculent* managed to issue a 'collision stations' alert, causing all hatches to be sealed, before the impact. The submarine sank within minutes. Ironically, the Captain and his Officer of the Watch and three lookouts in the conning tower, whose errors of judgment had placed the vessel in jeopardy, were saved by being thrown into the water. They were picked up quickly by a passing Dutch ship but were so incoherent with cold that for an hour no one suspected the magnitude of the tragedy. The Dutch vessel ploughed on up the river towards its destination at Gravesend, unaware of the catastrophe unfolding just beneath it.

The next miscalculation came on the *Truculent* itself. The senior officer left on board ordered an evacuation according to the rulebook. He was concerned that with the extra civilians on board, the increase in carbon dioxide in the atmosphere would be quicker than normal. Speed seemed to be of the essence. It was this judgment that turned out to be fatal for the crew.

It was a pitch perfect exercise, although it was discovered there were not enough lifejackets to go round. The crew decided that non-swimmers should have priority. The hatches were opened and, in all, 64 of the 74 trapped men managed to evacuate from the submarine. The problem was that, in the absence of any alert being raised, and the departure of the escort vessel earlier, there were no rescue ships to hand. The strong winter tides, and the freezing winter weather, caused the bulk of the escapees to perish by drowning or exposure. In hindsight, it was the speed of the evacuation that ironically condemned most of the men to their deaths. Just ten were picked up alive.

While press accounts the next day spoke in doom-laden terms of submariners entombed in their vessel, little did anyone realise the reality of what had transpired, and how avoidable the calamity had been. Most ironic of all, a disciplined and calmly orchestrated escape had unwittingly caused the worst loss of life since the war.

When the *Truculent* was raised two months later, just ten bodies were discovered in the vessel. In all, 64 men had died in the disaster, the vast majority having escaped but, due to the bizarre sequence of misfortunes, that escape turned out to be worst decision they could have made.

THE BIRTH OF THE GOODWIN SANDS

▪ *We end this chapter on accidents with perhaps the biggest and longest lasting of all, a celebrated – and often fiercely debated – piece of Kent folklore that was born on 3 November 1099: how the building of the church steeple at Tenterden inadvertently caused the disappearance of part of the county forty miles away, and led to the creation of the Goodwin Sands.*

Now visible to us only as an eleven-mile sandbank off the east coast of the county, nine centuries ago it was supposedly land, owned by the eminent Earl Godwine (or Goodwin), the county's most powerful landowner and father of King Harold, the beaten monarch at Hastings.

It was so low lying that it was protected against the sea by a high stone wall. According to the story, Goodwin had passed the land over to the care of the Abbot of St Augustine's at Canterbury, whose main aim in life, it seems, was to build a steeple at Tenterden. He devoted all his money and workers to the project and neglected the care and maintenance of the sea wall.

On the night of 3 November 1099, the sea came flooding over the wall, never to recede. A chronicler recorded the disaster as being 'occasioned by want of timely reparation to prevent the inundation of the sea which once getting in never recovered again.' Thus it is said that the Tenterden steeple was the cause of the creation of the Goodwin Sands.

A sizeable number of historians dispute the story, claiming that it was largely the invention of Sir Thomas More in the 16th century, and a similar story was in vogue in the 19th century linking the Sands and the building of the original Salisbury cathedral, which was completed in the same year as the great flood. Whatever the historical truth, the legend has endured, of the abbot who dreamed of leaving to posterity a memorable landmark and ended up bequeathing rather much more than he bargained for.

Down through history, the Sands have been one of the world's most notorious maritime hazards, responsible for many thousands of mishaps: in the region of 2,000 recorded wrecks (and probably a lot more unknown) and tens of thousands of deaths in shipping disasters down the centuries. It would fill another book to document the many accidents the Sands have caused – in spite of the variety of individual circumstances, this is largely a long, sorry tale of dreary monotony. Instead, we will return to the Sands in Chapter 6 when we highlight some of the many extraordinary attempts, often themselves ending in disaster, to make them a safer place.

4

UNSOLVED MYSTERIES

BRITAIN'S GREATEST LOST TREASURE

■ *The famed shrine of St Thomas Becket in Canterbury Cathedral was renowned as the English church's most prestigious religious relic. The entire treasure disappeared without trace on the orders of Henry VIII during one of the worst excesses of the Reformation in England.*

FOR THREE CENTURIES the shrine had been the centrepiece of a pilgrim's visit to Canterbury. Becket's remains had been re-interred there in the main body of the cathedral fifty years after his death. It became traditional that visitors made donations to the shrine. Over time, hundreds of foreign dignitaries had adorned it with spectacular offerings and it quickly far surpassed all other shrines in Christendom in value and beauty. At its height it was described as being 'wholly covered with plates of gold, yet the gold is scarcely seen because it is covered with various precious stones, as sapphires, diamonds, rubies, emeralds and wherever the eye turns something more beautiful than the rest is observed.'

Erasmus described it shortly before its destruction: 'The least valuable portion was gold; every part glistened and shone and sparkled with rare and very large jewels, some of them exceeding the size of a goose's egg.' A celebrated offering was a cup of pure gold left by Louis VII of France (described by a chronicler as 'a much prized gem'). At the same time Louis made the monks an annual grant of 1,600 gallons of French wine, which must, no doubt, have been an even more prized gem. In one year in the early 13th century, money offerings amounted to £320. In today's values, that is in the order of a quarter of a million pounds.

The last person known to have viewed the shrine was a French noblewoman, Madame de Montreuil, who, with the French ambassador, visited the cathedral on 31 August 1538. Sometime during September 1538, at the height of the dissolution of the monasteries, the entire collection was seized by the king. The treasure filled two enormous chests, each one needing eight men to lift it. A spectacular procession of 26 wagons loaded with loot pulled out of the cathedral and the treasure disappeared forever.

Official records assessed the gold taken from the shrine at almost 5,000 ounces, along with 4,500 ounces of gilt plate, 840 ounces of panel gilt and almost 5,300 ounces of plain silver. In modern terms, that would be worth some £3 million. All the records relating to the disposal of the treasure were destroyed. No one knows how or where it all ended up.

Two months later Henry issued a proclamation making Thomas Becket a 'non-person'. He was declared a traitor and orders were given that every picture, image or statue to him was to be destroyed. He could not be mentioned, named, reported or called a saint. The records and legal documents of the cathedral were systematically and rigorously weeded and Becket's name carefully deleted. It amounted to the most comprehensive attempt to expunge an individual from history and its like was not seen again until the days of Communist manipulation of history in the 20th century.

The ransacking of the shrine also created mystery and controversy over what happened to the remains of Becket's body. When he was assassinated (see Chapter 7), the monks were said to have immediately buried him in an obscure part of the cathedral to prevent the expected desecration by the king. The body had been moved fifty years after his death to rest in the new shrine but what the fate of the bones was after its destruction has been a source of intrigue ever since. In the absence of any record from that day of what had been done with the bones, the assumed version of events has been that the monks of the time managed to squirrel them away and rebury them elsewhere in the cathedral for safekeeping. But no one knew for sure where.

There was excitement in Victorian times when archaeologists claimed to have found them in the crypt in 1888. There are records of a forensic examination, which proved inconclusive as to whether the skull had damage consistent with the description of Becket's injuries. The bones were then reburied where they had been found.

They remained undisturbed until 1949 when a second exhumation was conducted for another scientific study, by a professor of anatomy from St Bartholomew's Hospital and an anthropologist from Cambridge. The whole affair was carried out in great secrecy and word did not emerge of it until two years later. Reports circulating in 1951 said that the inspection had 'conclusively discounted' the possibility that the bones were Becket's, relying primarily on the discrepancies surrounding the fractures to the skull as the main grounds for the conclusion. So the recovery of what many would consider to be the greatest sacred relic of the English church continues to be unresolved.

A VICTORIAN TRAGEDY

■ *Having a tangential link with the county, one of the Victorian era's greatest exploration disasters was planned and resourced in the county.*

On 26 July 1845, the last sighting by British eyes of the ill-fated Franklin expedition signalled the beginning of the century's longest-running mystery of exploration. Franklin was endeavouring to find the famed North-West Passage through the scattered islands of the Canadian Arctic to the Pacific Ocean. The disappearance without trace of the two-ship team, together with 134 officers and men, led to one of the longest sustained public campaigns for government assistance to help find the missing seamen. It was to be fourteen years before any hint of their fate emerged.

The trip had begun in highly optimistic vein, in May, when Sir John Franklin, a veteran explorer-navigator, had accepted the task of putting together another attempt to find the Passage – the 58th. He made his base Greenhithe and it was there in the first five months of 1845 that feverish preparations were made for the expedition.

Franklin lodged at the White Hart Inn and on 18 May the pair of ships, the *Erebus* and the *Terror*, loosed their moorings and sailed down the Thames. Two months later they were last spotted by an Aberdeen whaling boat in Lancaster Sound, at the northern tip of Canada's Baffin Island. They were never seen again.

Two years of complete silence passed and public anxiety began to mount. Franklin's wife spent every penny she had over the next ten years lobbying the government to send out a rescue mission and financing searches of her own. In the end the authorities confined themselves to putting up a £20,000 prize for his successful rescue.

As the years passed, it became £10,000 just for word of him. In all, an astronomical 39 expeditions tried to find Franklin. None succeeded. At the peak of the national frenzy between 1847 and 1852 the Admiralty became deluged with petitions about the affair and it was hardly ever out of the newspapers. Every year or so a titbit of the jigsaw would be discovered – traces of a ship here, a stack of discarded tins of meat there.

Gradually the story emerged, helped dramatically by the testimony in 1854 of an official of the Hudson's Bay Company who told of a meeting with a party of Eskimo who claimed to have seen white men travelling in the ice of King William Island well to the west of Baffin. He had obtained the trinkets that the Eskimo had been given for food, and they contained a silver plate engraved with 'Sir John F'. It was the first solid evidence of the party for almost a decade.

Five years later an expedition came across remnants of a ship, a few skeletons and some clothes. They returned to England with a metal canister they had found buried in a cairn. It contained the account – dated April 1848 – by Captain Crozier, second in command, which told the bare facts of the fateful tale. It recounted that fourteen months after the last sighting they became trapped in ice and drifted barely thirty miles in two years. Sir John Franklin had died in June 1847 and 23 other crew members had also perished to date. Crozier had just decided to abandon the ships and they were about to start on foot in an attempt to reach safety. No one made it.

Ironically Franklin had technically achieved his aim. The location of his team's final position given in the note showed that he had sailed further west than a point another English ship had already reached coming from the opposite direction. The two routes had overlapped, proving there was a way through. It was not until the 1980s that the remains of the sailors buried near the cairn were rediscovered, perfectly preserved by the permafrost in exactly the condition as the day they died. The poignant note telling of Franklin's fate is preserved too – in the National Maritime Museum in Greenwich, a few miles from where his doomed voyage started out.

BRITAIN'S WORST MASS MURDERER?

▮ *Could a series of catastrophic explosions thought to be accidents in fact have been the work of a mass murderer?*

One of the great First World War naval mysteries began with the cataclysmic destruction on 26 November 1914 of HMS *Bulwark* while moored at Sheerness. Shortly before 8 o'clock that morning, the warship was obliterated by a gigantic explosion, possibly the most deadly to have happened in Britain's waters. The deadline for return after leave had passed barely an hour earlier, so the entire complement of the ship was on board, and at that time of the morning most were below decks at breakfast. It is thought that up to 730 men were killed; there were just 14 survivors. The explosion was heard as far away as Rainham, and windows were rattled in Southend across the estuary.

At the time, the tragedy was unexplained and put down to one of those unfortunate accidents that occur in wartime, but later events caused investigators to look at the incident with fresh eyes.

Six months later, on 27 May 1915, again at Sheerness, another ship blew up, again without warning or explanation. The minelayer *Princess Irene* was lost, along with 170 of her crew and 76 dockyard workers who were on board. The explosion was so extreme that part of the ship's boiler landed on another ship more than half a mile away. Places ten miles to the south were covered with falling debris. There were reports of people being injured by shrapnel as far away as Sittingbourne, and a nine-year-old girl was killed on the Isle of Grain when she was struck by a fragment. Again, the official conclusion drawn was that it had been a terrible accident.

Two more ships that, like the first pair, were officially based at Chatham, then suffered similar fates. Seven months on – 30 December 1915 – and the *Natal* blew up mysteriously off Invergordon in Scotland with the loss of 428 crew. Then on 9 July 1917, the last of the mystery four – the *Vanguard* – blew up in Scapa Flow, taking 843 of her crew down. Only two sailors were saved.

The sequence attracted the suspicions of the Admiralty. Investigations uncovered a link between all four and a weapons fitter, John Harston. He had been employed on both the *Natal* and the *Vanguard* at the time of their loss. As a Chatham-based seaman, he had had easy access to the others, which had both just come from the shipyard to their Sheerness moorings when they destroyed themselves.

The link had been discovered during the enquiry into the loss of the *Natal* when it was found that Harston had been on board the ship all day until 11.15 pm on the night of the explosion. He had left less than an hour before it blew up. He aroused suspicion because of his apparent lack of basic knowledge about the layout of the ship on which he had been serving for several months. From this apparent wish to cover up what he knew of the ship the trail led back to Chatham and the other ships.

Although further investigations were pursued, no substantive evidence ever emerged to implicate Harston – just a curious string of deadly coincidences which, if true, would make John Harston, with over 2,200 deaths to his name, one of history's greatest mass killers.

THE MYSTERIOUS DEATH OF A FLYING LEGEND

■ *Amy Johnson, Britain's most famous aviation heroine, is presumed to have died when her plane crashed into the Thames off Chatham in January 1941. The circumstances surrounding the accident, however, were shrouded in wartime secrecy, and have never been fully disclosed.*

AMY JOHNSON: SHE FLEW THE WORLD.

Amy Johnson was one of those pioneers who personified the daredevil 1930s in British aviation. She was the first British woman to qualify as an aircraft engineer. In May 1930, aged just 26 and despite never having flown farther than from her native Hull to London, she made the first flight to Australia, catapulting herself to national and world fame, as well as receiving a CBE and £10,000 from the *Daily Mail*. It was the first of many long-distance flights in the 1930s, including record times to Tokyo and Cape Town.

Her exploits had become legendary. Her death on 5 January 1941, however, became forever shrouded in mystery and confusion.

She was in wartime service working as a ferry pilot for the Air Transport Auxiliary. On that gloomy winter's day, she was supposedly flying solo to an undisclosed destination when her plane ditched in the river near Chatham in mid-afternoon. The aircraft was seen to crash by a passing Royal Navy vessel and a figure was spotted baling out. A few moments later, a speedboat was on the scene and a Lt Col Fletcher dived into the water and swam towards someone in the water.

It is here that the mystery begins. Initial accounts from some of those on the boat maintained that they saw two figures in the water, a man and a woman. The woman, presumed to be Johnson, quickly disappeared beneath the waves. Despite heroic efforts, Fletcher had no success either with saving his target, the man. Fletcher himself was pulled from the water nearly unconscious from exposure. He died within hours. He was the only man who might have known the identity of whoever it was he tried to save.

There was no official statement from the authorities for three days.

When one did come, it added to the confusion. Authorisation papers found in the vicinity of the accident appeared to confirm that the aircraft was indeed Johnson's. The government, however, said that Johnson had left Blackpool at 10.45 that morning for a flight to Oxfordshire scheduled to take just an hour. She was carrying no passengers. She had reported bad weather shortly after take-off and then nothing more had been heard from her after her last words, 'Right, I'm going over the top' (meaning flying over the storm clouds), until she ditched at 3.30 in the afternoon a hundred miles off her supposed course.

Her machine carried enough fuel for 4¾ hours, almost five times that necessary for the purported flight and exactly the time that had elapsed between take-off and crash. The official version being put together was that she had become disorientated due to the bad weather and had flown in circles completely lost for over four hours before simply running out of fuel.

This explanation has provoked endless scepticism. For a pilot of Johnson's skill and experience over vastly more treacherous and uncharted territory, it seems hardly credible that she could have remained lost so ineptly for so long. Inevitably, other theories have mushroomed, particularly after the reported sighting of a passenger, raising the possibility of some secret mission to the Continent that came to grief on its return to England. Other suggestions have included that she was secretly transporting a foreign spy out of the country, possibly her lover; that she was accidentally shot down by friendly fire, an admission too embarrassing for the government to confess to given her worldwide fame (an ex-wartime anti-aircraft gunner claimed this in 1999); and that it was an elaborate plan to fake her death so that she could start a new life (a claim made by her former mechanic, also in 1999).

At the inquest held at Chatham into Lt Col Fletcher's death, an Air Ministry official scotched rumours of a passenger and maintained that the second 'person' was simply Johnson's parachute backpack floating in the water. Only Fletcher would know whether he had tried to save a person or a parachute, and he was conveniently dead. He now lies buried in Woodlands cemetery, Gillingham, his secret with him. No bodies were ever officially found. Johnson's death was legally presumed at a special Probate Court hearing in December 1943, nearly three years after the accident.

In 2002, a retired naval clerk who was on duty at the speedboat's shore station that morning added the latest twist to the tale. He claimed to have been told immediately afterwards by one of the rescue team that the person in the water had indeed identified themselves as Amy Johnson. A rope was thrown to her, but she had not been able to reach it. A member of the crew dashed to the helm and threw the boat's engines into reverse and tried to close in on her. But as they neared, she was drawn into the propellers and chopped to pieces. The rescuer was long dead, so the story could not be corroborated.

Perhaps, then, the real reason for the enduring mystery has been nothing more sinister than to cover up causing the death of the most famous aviator in the world. Who would care to admit to that?

However plausible this new version of events that day may be, to some there will still always be the unanswered question of how Johnson came to fall out of the sky over the Thames in the first place. For that, there has never been any convincing explanation.

MYSTERY DEATH OF A MUSICIAN

■ *American band leader Glenn Miller disappeared over the county on the afternoon of 15 December 1944 in one of the world's greatest and enduring aviation mysteries.*

Theories abound as to what actually happened to Glenn Miller, some of which are bizarre in the extreme. Some claim he was never on the plane at all, that he was in fact an enemy spy whose cover had been blown and the flight had had to be faked either to cover his own escape to Germany or Russia or to hide his elimination by the Allied authorities. Some say he arrived safely at his destination in Paris but was killed in a brawl over a prostitute in the city's red light district and the fiction of an air crash was invented to protect his image. 'Witnesses' have been found who testify both to seeing him land at another British airfield shortly after his official take-off and to seeing him safely in Paris. In 1974 a marine explorer claimed to have found the wreckage of the aircraft in the Channel twelve miles off Dymchurch but nothing conclusive ever came of the reported find. In 1983, Miller's brother, Herb, claimed that the bandleader had died of cancer shortly after arriving in Paris.

There is an even more incredible claim that Miller had died in Ohio from gun shot wounds in 1945 after being flown back there from Europe to an American air base for surgery after being shot during an attempt by German special forces to kill or kidnap General Eisenhower, who was then based in Paris and defending the fragile Allied lines against the German counter attack of the Battle of the Bulge. The theory goes that Eisenhower had summoned Miller to instruct him to do some propaganda broadcasts to Germany.

What is undisputed is that Miller and his manager set off from an airfield at Bedford around lunchtime that foggy Friday for the trip to Paris in advance of the rest of the band whose larger aircraft was unable to take off in the poor weather. They were all en route to make a live radio broadcast on Christmas Day from liberated Paris as a morale-boosting show for the forces.

The trip was shrouded in elaborate secrecy. Miller, who was under contract to the BBC to perform a large number of live concerts and radio shows (which had become an outstandingly popular series since they began shortly after D-Day in June that year) had unusually recorded six weeks' worth of 'live' shows in advance so that listeners would have no inkling of the Paris extravaganza until the day it happened. His purportedly live shows continued to go out from the BBC while the band packed and made ready for shipping themselves across to France. The shows continued to run for ten days after his disappearance while the authorities deliberated with increasing anxiety how to break the news.

Sometime in mid-afternoon the plane crossed Kent and headed out over the Channel (it is assumed). Nothing more is certain. His disappearance was curiously not noticed until his band arrived in Paris three days later and were surprised not to be met by their leader. Anxious enquiries revealed that no one had expected, or seen, him earlier.

GLENN MILLER: THERE ARE AT LEAST HALF A DOZEN THEORIES ABOUT HIS ULTIMATE FATE.

Meanwhile, having unwittingly made the announcement of the Christmas Day spectacular, the authorities were in a dilemma. Not knowing his whereabouts (his appearance, for example, on German radio in response to an announcement that he had died would have been a tumultuous propaganda victory for the enemy) they prevaricated for as long as they could.

On Christmas Eve, the day before the show, they were forced to announce his disappearance. Nothing came in response from Germany and the mystery then started in earnest, eventually producing the official conclusion that his plane had hit mechanical trouble, possibly due to iced-up wings, and had come down in the Channel.

That scenario seemed to have been substantiated thirty years later with the presumed discovery of the wreckage in 200 ft of water off the Kent coast, but nothing conclusive could be recovered to end the speculation once and for all. Another diver, in 1985, claimed positive identification of Miller's craft 'off the coast of France', suggesting a different location. This showed no damage to the craft, and no sign of any human remains. Again, it could only feed speculation.

Another bizarre theory had by then emerged. In 1984 a retired US Air Force navigator claimed that Miller's plane was the accidental victim of an Allied bomber jettisoning its ordnance as it returned from an aborted mission over the Continent. His Lancaster was flying three times higher than Miller's craft and would never have spotted it as it released its 4,000 lb blast bombs in a designated jettison area in the Channel from which all other aircraft were supposedly prohibited. The new theory was that Miller ventured by mistake into the danger area and was hit by the falling bomb. Such a theory would explain, its proponents say, the absence of any substantial pieces of wreckage.

The Ministry of Defence's Air Historical Branch investigated the claim and, while not being able to confirm that this was the definitive answer because no formal mission report had been filed by the Lancaster as the mission had technically been aborted, the research could not find any evidence to contradict the claim. In 2000, further supporting evidence surfaced in the shape of the plane's log-book which appeared to confirm the navigator's account of the jettisoning of the surplus bombs.

The mystery is unlikely ever to be resolved conclusively, nor will the tantalising prospect ever diminish of recovering the remains. Miller is said to have been carrying a briefcase stocked full of new and hitherto unheard compositions for the Christmas show. It is the chance of discovering these that will ensure that the search will go on.

More mysteries of the Channel

■ *London's* Globe *newspaper reported on 13 December 1919 the discovery of Kent's own* Marie Celeste, *a deserted ship found beached on the Goodwin Sands.*

The ship was identified as a French ketch, the *Lucienne*, whose home port was St Malo in Brittany, far to the west down the Channel. It was carrying a cargo of cement and when found there was no one on board although the ship itself was completely undamaged. All its sails were set out and intact and the ship's wheel was lashed with rope to keep it on one particular course. In the cabin below, there were the remains of a meal and signs that the crew had made a rapid departure as several items of clothing were strewn around the decks.

But the whereabouts of the crew was a complete mystery. It was believed that there were six of them and the official investigation concluded that for some reason they had taken to the ship's small auxiliary boat somewhere in the Channel and that the *Lucienne* had sailed on its pre-set course, abandoned and uncontrolled, up the Channel until it hit the Sands. There is no record of the crew ever being found or a solution to the mystery ever being discovered.

The *Lucienne* was not the only ghost ship connected with Kent to have come to light. Another mysterious candidate was the barge *Zebrina*, built at Faversham in 1873. For most of her career she plied the coastal waters unspectacularly, but she saw action off South America when for a time she was used to transport raw materials between and around the Brazilian and Argentinian coasts. She came back to Europe shortly before the outbreak of the First World War. What would turn out to be her last voyage began from Falmouth in Cornwall in October 1917, laden with coal for the short cross-Channel trip to St Brieuc, again in Brittany and just 40 miles from St Malo, the home port of the *Lucienne*.

Two days after sailing and when she had been several hours overdue, a search revealed her whereabouts, beached at Rozel Point, south of Cherbourg and many miles off course. There was no apparent damage to the ship and not a soul to be found on board. Nothing was ever heard of the crew again.

No connection between the two events has ever been made but the mystery deepens when one considers that a third abandoned, apparently undamaged and fully rigged ship, the *Marion Douglas*, was found off the Scilly Isles just a fortnight before the *Lucienne*; the crew had vanished. How, it was not clear since the ship's motor launch was still tied to the stern.

UNNATURAL PHENOMENA

■ *Some strange events are easier to explain than others.*

Kent has suffered numerous freak inflictions of weather but probably none more so than the events of 1 November 1755 when a curious phenomenon was recorded at Tenterden and places nearby. Between ten and eleven that morning, the waters of several streams and ponds were, in the words of a contemporary account, 'forced up the banks with great violence, foaming, fretting and roaring like the coming in of the tide so as to frighten many that were near.' In some cases, the water rose and fell three times during the morning. Other sightings reported the water circling in foaming eddies and whirlpools.

Although unexplained at the time, the date reveals the probable cause: a thousand miles away, at 9.30 that morning, one of the largest and most devastating earthquakes ever to hit Europe struck the Portuguese coast, completely destroying Lisbon and killing over 50,000 people. The shock waves ran far and wide. A 50 ft wave surge reached Cornwall and at the other end of the Channel ships broke their anchor chains in Rotterdam harbour.

The villagers of Tenterden and elsewhere in the county witnessed a frightening but comparatively harmless effect of the distant monumental catastrophe.

Other meteorological experiences have been less easy to explain. On 18 December 1741, a chronicler recorded that at about noon a large ball of fire was seen to pass over Canterbury; this was followed by a storm which broke almost every window in the city. The following morning three suns appeared in the sky along with an inverted rainbow, which lasted from nine o'clock until noon 'to the great astonishment of the inhabitants'. No explanation has ever been advanced.

In November 1803, a 'vivid meteor' was reported at Gillingham accompanied by a noise similar to the sound of an artillery cannon being fired. It was so universally heard in the Medway that hundreds of people fled from their houses, thinking that the invasion alarm guns were being fired. The concussion was so great that it shook ships at anchor in the river. It is anyone's guess as to what in reality occurred that day.

The weirdest story on record comes from *Otio Imperialia*, the chronicle of Gervase of Tilbury, which is an account dating from 1211 when a mysterious 'ship in the clouds' dropped anchor in a

Gravesend churchyard, apparently by accident because men 'swam' down the anchor cables to try to free the ship, couldn't, so cut them and the ship 'sailed' on. Reputedly a local blacksmith used the abandoned anchor to make an ornamental lectern for the church. This could be one of the earliest recorded sightings of a UFO, but we are never likely to know for certain what the locals saw that day in Gravesend.

THE FIRST UFO?

■ *A frightening event which caused mass panic in the Medway has never been explained. It represents the first UFO sighting officially acknowledged by British authorities.*

Winston Churchill, at the time First Lord of the Admiralty, answered a question in the House of Commons on 21 November 1912 that constitutes the first official government statement recorded on the subject of Unidentified Flying Objects. It concerned an unexplained incident five weeks before, over Sheerness, which came to be known as the 'Sheerness Scare'. The local paper headlined it 'The Nightmare'. These were truly fearsome days for Kent's populace.

No explanation has ever been offered for what happened over the town on the night of 14 October that year. What is known is that between 6.30 and 7 pm a strange buzzing sound was heard in the air over Sheerness by a vast number of residents. The area was not unused to such sounds since the whole of the Isle of Sheppey was a pioneering testing ground for aircraft in the early days of flight. Flares were lit at Eastchurch four miles away to guide whatever was up there down but nothing landed.

The locals began to panic, thinking that they had been visited by a German Zeppelin airship. The craft were then in their infancy and had never yet been seen over Britain and were subject to much fearful rumour in the days of increasing international tension.

Questions were asked in the House and Churchill gave the government's considered reply after making enquiries. He recounted the facts that it was beyond doubt that many hundreds of Sheerness witnesses had heard the loud noises but that no aircraft made a landing. There was no evidence to indicate the nationality of the aircraft but it was confirmed that it was 'not one of ours'. That was the sum of the official statement.

Further local investigations established that no German craft had been in the area that night. The nearest Zeppelin was over the German island of Heligoland, almost 400 miles away. (Given also that the Zeppelin was believed to be over 500 ft long, the local paper observed, it seemed incredible that anyone could believe that such a ship could pass over Sheerness when the look-out men on the ships in the harbour, the signalmen at Garrison Point Fort, the coastguards patrolling the shores and the police on duty all stated that nothing had been seen that night.) It had also been established that it could not have been a British aircraft on a night flight from Eastchurch – none had been in the air that evening.

Little more is ever likely to be known about the tantalising incident. Zeppelins were certainly in existence but it is doubtful that they could make the long trip across the North Sea undetected. We shall never know, but could the 'Sheerness Scare' be the first officially acknowledged and documented UFO sighting in Britain? Many modern investigators believe it is precisely that.

5

WICKED NATURE

KENT EARTHQUAKES

▌ *It may surprise many, but Kent is not unknown for being hit by earthquakes. History records more than a dozen significant events, the earliest hitting Canterbury in AD 483, the last as recently as the April 2007 event that shook Folkestone. Although impossible to measure scientifically, the damage recorded in the Great Kent Earthquake of 6 April 1580 suggests that it was the strongest to have hit anywhere in Britain up to that time. It has probably only been surpassed by the 'Great English Earthquake' of 1884 that struck Colchester and which may have killed up to four people.*

WHILE THERE WERE no recorded deaths in the county from the 1580 event, one person was killed by falling masonry as far away as London. The coastal regions suffered worst. The tremors, of which three were felt during the day, culminated in the big shock around six o'clock in the evening which caused the sea to foam and swell and ships at Sandwich 'tottered'. At Dover, part of the cliff and the castle wall fell into the sea and a section of Saltwood castle near Hythe collapsed. The bells of Hythe church were heard to ring of their own accord. The old church of St Mary's in Sandwich was nearly completely destroyed and St Peter's was badly damaged. The tower at St Peter's in Broadstairs still bears a large crack that has been attributed to the earthquake.

The quake was described as being accompanied by 'a marvellous great noise as though the shot of some great battery of a number of cannons was going off at the same instant.' The sound seemed to come from mid-Channel. So widespread was the disaster that a special prayer was issued to churches asking God to avert his wrath.

At sea, a passenger travelling out from Dover reported that his vessel had touched the sea bed five times and that the sea had risen into the air more than 40 ft above them. In all, some 120 ships were said to have been lost in the Channel.

There was another severe tremor three weeks later about midnight on 1 May. This one was centred on the Ashford area but was felt as far afield as Gravesend and Dover. According to the historian Stow, it 'caused the inhabitants to rise from their beds and run to their churches where they called upon God in earnest prayer to be merciful to them.'

At least twelve other earthquakes are recorded in the county's history. The earliest, in AD 483, has little further descriptive detail other than its location being at Canterbury. In 1246 a tremor 'overturn'd several churches' around Canterbury and again in 1382 Canterbury was the epicentre. This one shattered windows in the cathedral and caused the bell tower to collapse. One in 1596 'did great damage to buildings and killed several people' and one in 1692 off the coast caused considerable destruction in Deal and Sandwich. Sizeable tremors, in the low fours on the modern Richter scale, occurred in 1776 and 1950. Canterbury was again the centre of two strong tremors, in 1931 and 1933. In 1936, villages such as Snowdown and Adisham, south-east of the city, experienced a tremor that caused inhabitants to flee in the streets. The 2007 event in Folkestone damaged 1,500 homes. We're not as immune as we often like to think.

WEIRD AND WICKED WEATHER

■ *Down the centuries, the elements have inflicted many disasters on Kent and its people. Here we document some of the worst, and many of the strangest, occurrences.*

The deepest freeze
The worst day of the worst winter on record in Kent was 12 January 1779. The Thames, which had been frozen further upriver since mid-

December, froze at Sheerness on this day, forming a continuous sheet of ice from the Isle of Sheppey over to the Essex coast. The river had never before – nor ever since – frozen so far down the estuary, where it is five and a half miles wide.

Eyewitnesses recorded that it was possible to drive a carriage a mile out from the shore. The Swale, separating Sheppey from the mainland, had been frozen since 17 December. People regularly walked to and from the island. The icebound King's Ferry would not resume sailings until 19 January, one of the longest freezes on record.

The driest drought
In October 1134, the county was suffering a great drought. It was so hot on the 6th that the Medway completely dried up at Rochester and, for the only time in recorded history, people were able to walk from one side to the other.

Wicked storms
Freak storms have been regularly recorded. In 1287, a storm described by the chroniclers as a tempest blew in from the Channel and devastated Romney Marsh. Sand and shingle up to a depth of 3 ft covered New Romney. The marks are still said to be visible on the pillars of St Nicholas' church in the town.

The gale that blew in on 9 November 1800 struck most of the southern counties and destroyed hundreds of buildings but in Kent it caused one of the most bizarre accidents on record. A windmill at Frindsbury, near Strood, was destroyed when it caught fire from the friction generated by being blown round in the hurricane force winds. It was totally burned out.

The weirdest weather year
Kent was prominent with some freak weather on the afternoon of 9 August 1911 as Canterbury broke the British temperature record with an official reading of 98.2°F in the shade. Two other places shared the feat, Epsom in Surrey and Raunds in Northamptonshire, as the country sweltered in the hottest summer on record.

That year had been an odd one all round for weather. An exceptionally mild winter had produced no snow at all for the first time in living memory. Then blizzards struck southern England in April with snow lying several feet deep across the northern slopes of the Downs near Chatham and Sittingbourne. A mail coach trying to get from Maidstone to Chatham took six hours to cover the seven miles. Temperatures stayed below freezing for days in the arctic spring.

Then, less than three months later, Kent saw the other extreme. Local accounts speak of the entire county being scorched brown by September after three months of unremitting sun. True to British form, the weather dominated the columns of the local press. In Maidstone the writers of the local paper bewailed in the lead article: 'We are helpless in the face of the heat. At four o'clock in the afternoon the thermometer is standing at 90° in the room looking east [i.e., away from the sun] in which we are writing and at 125° [out of shade] on the roof above us.' It helpfully provided almost an entire page of advice about sea bathing and passed on the equally enticing news 'from an Eastern paper' that 'there was a beautiful custom in Japan whereby the wife, during the hot weather, sits up all night fanning the fevered brow of her husband.'

The Canterbury record stood for 79 years until 3 August 1990 when a reading of 98.8° was taken in Cheltenham. Kent regained the record in 2003 when Brogdale, near Faversham recorded 101.3° on 10 August.

Summer ice storms

For pure meteorological anarchy, though, nothing can surpass the bizarre storm that struck Tunbridge Wells at the height of the summer in 1956. On August Bank Holiday Monday an unprecedented hail and ice storm turned the streets of the town into an arctic wasteland for an afternoon. Dumbstruck passers-by could only look on in disbelief as what had been a cool and overcast summer's day became a frozen downpour. Ice accumulated in the roads and brought traffic to a standstill.

The debris from the storm was picturesquely described by the local paper as appearing like 'a rice pudding spreading throughout the town'. Roofs collapsed because of the weight of ice and a press photographer captured an immortal picture of a bus and motor car marooned in what appeared to be a snow drift. The image was splashed on the front page – under a dateline of August.

It later took over a hundred lorry loads to clear the ice from the town. The storm was remarkably isolated – few outside the town were aware of the calamity falling within in. At Tonbridge, only five miles away to the north, the weather was reported to be fine and quite normal.

THE Great Storm

The most deadly storm ever to hit southern England blew up the Channel on 27 November 1703, leaving an unprecedented trail of death and destruction. Although similar in form to our more recent experience in 1987, the Great Blow of 1703 outranked all before or since for the sheer scale of death it caused. The Royal Navy lost an entire battle fleet of 13 ships, which had been moored off Dover. It is the greatest single loss it has ever suffered, even in battle. Another 300 merchant ships went down. Accounts speak of upwards of 30,000 sailors being lost in the Channel and it is thought that over a thousand people on land were killed.

The storm had been blowing for a fortnight but it reached its peak around 6 am that day. The captain of the HMS *Association*, lying off Dover, witnessed the full force of the wind 'skimming up the water as if it had been sand and carrying it into the air.' His ship survived, but it was blown right across the North Sea to Norway.

A seaman by the name of Thomas Atkins had a remarkable escape. His ship, the *Mary*, was blown onto the Goodwin Sands. He was the only survivor from a crew of 270, mainly because he was clinging to the mast at the time and as the ship was blown almost horizontal he jumped onto another ship which was passing. Later in the same night, that ship too sank and Atkins was again among the survivors.

At Cranbrook, 16 miles inland, the earth was so salted by sea spray that cattle refused to eat the grass for weeks. At St Peter's in Broadstairs, a cow was found still alive in the highest branches of a tree. A boat was blown 275 yards inland at Whitstable and the North

Foreland lighthouse, which was then an open-topped coal brazier, showered cinders for miles around, setting fire to hundreds of thatched roofs.

The tallest steeple in the county, that at Brenchley, collapsed. Reputed to have been over 160 ft tall, it was levelled to the ground, bringing down most of the rest of the church too. It was reported later that children played on the rubble so as to claim that they had jumped over the highest spire in Kent.

The celebrated writer Daniel Defoe carried out his own personal survey of the destruction and published what became the only comprehensive record of the day. In Kent, he personally counted 17,000 fallen oaks 'then gave up counting as it seemed pointless and wearisome to do so.' He reported seeing roof tiles flying 50 yards and embedding themselves in the ground by up to eight inches. 'Most people expected the fall of their houses. And yet, nobody dared quit their tottering habitations: for whatever the danger was within doors, it was worse without.'

Much like the 1987 storm, there were always some who profited. Defoe reported that the price of new roof tiles had rocketed from £2 10s a thousand to £6. It was to be another ten generations before another visitation remotely resembling this event would come Kent's way again.

KENT'S TORNADO

■ *Next in order of the greatest and freakiest storms to hit Kent – if not the whole country – blew up the Channel on 19 August 1763 and cut a swathe of destruction forty miles long through the county. Kent's very own tornado – hardly any damage was done elsewhere – struck, in the words of a contemporary, 'with a terror not easily expressed'.*

The storm came ashore on the Sussex coast and wreaked its havoc along a narrow path five miles wide, crossing the border at Tunbridge Wells and heading north-east on a path taking it through Pembury, Paddock Wood, Maidstone and out to sea again near Sheerness.

An eyewitness account speaks of the fateful day starting as

suffocatingly hot with scarcely a breath of air. At 10 in the morning there was noticed a deepening black fringe of cloud on the western horizon which closed in with incredible velocity, accompanied by thunder that became a continuous roar. By 11.30 am it was raining torrentially and large hailstones were falling. There was general panic as the storm swept through while others stood 'like inanimate beings', dumbfounded at the sight.

A scene of universal desolation was described with uprooted trees, orchards stripped of fruit, houses and barns flattened and water pouring in torrents down the streets. Animals lay dead in the fields, struck down by the fist-sized hailstones. In Maidstone, buildings on one side of the High Street had all their windows shattered by the hail, which was so fierce that the wooden latticed frames were also forced in.

The hail was the most remarkable feature of the storm, which nowhere lasted much more than half an hour. Huge fragments were recovered. At Barming, south of Maidstone, a piece was found which the local parish vicar – presumably a reliable source – measured at 9 inches round. Even ten days after the storm, hailstones measuring 4½ inches across were still being found.

Maidstone was hit worst. After Detling, the hillsides absorbed most of the rest of the fury and it died away back over the coast. For days the 'corridor of terror' became a magnet for sightseers who travelled from wide around to witness the scenes. Nothing like it was to be seen again until the events of 1987.

THE NORTH SEA SURGE

■ *On the night of 31 January 1953, the east coast of England was devastated by some of the worst flooding in Britain's history. A number of extreme weather events combined to create a tidal surge, which caused major flooding in areas along the coasts of Essex, Norfolk, Suffolk, Kent and the outer Thames Estuary: 307 people died, 24,000 homes were damaged or destroyed and over 40,000 people were evacuated. Miraculously, in Kent only one death was recorded. Damage in monetary terms was estimated at over £5 billion in modern values.*

WATER POURS THROUGH A BREACH IN KENT'S DEFENCES
AT ERITH DURING THE 1953 FLOODS.

As far as Kent was concerned, the story of the great East Coast Floods of 1953 was more one of narrow escape than of tragedy and disaster. Norfolk and Essex bore the brunt, particularly Canvey Island across the Thames Estuary from Kent where a fifth of all deaths occurred.

But damage and disruption in the county was immense. The 700 acres of Belvedere marshes near Woolwich (then very much still part of Kent) were inundated, washing away the caravan homes of 300 people. Half the Isle of Sheppey was under water, and Sheerness cut off. The Royal Army Service Corps laid on a ferry service between Chatham and Sheerness to supply milk and food to the devastated island. A coach load of passengers had to be rescued near the King's Ferry Bridge linking the island with the mainland, having spent a terrified night in the vehicle with the floodwaters rising around them. Gravesend was badly affected by flooding.

The coastline gave way along the Thanet coast, causing severe damage to Herne Bay and to Whitstable's famous oyster beds. When the next season began that September, it was estimated that 20 per cent of the catch was dead, thought to be as a result of the heavy deposits of salt. Faversham was cut off and several miles of the railway line linking the string of Thanet towns was washed away.

Of the Kent River Board's 120-mile length of sea and river defence responsibility, all but a stretch of three miles had been topped by the surge. Officials of the board called it 'the greatest disaster that had occurred in the county for centuries'. Over 50,000 acres eventually flooded, many to depths of 8–9 ft. Remarkably, most damage was repaired within a fortnight and withstood a major storm that followed on 16 February. Perhaps more characteristically, the North Kent rail line, linking London to Ramsgate, which was also put out of action by the deluge, did not get back to normal use until early June.

One of the strangest of sights as the county cleared up was the use by servicemen from Nore Command of amphibious landing craft to rescue some of the thousands of stranded cattle and sheep.

The floods gave the impetus to the building of the Thames Barrier defence at Charlton, which opened in 1984. As any resident east of that point readily realises, the core purpose of the defence is its protection of central London – by dispersing any flood tide into the Essex and north Kent coastlines. Dartford, Gravesend, the Isle of Grain and the Medway towns are designated to be the sacrifice.

In 2005, having in mind the new town developments planned in the Thames Gateway regeneration scheme, the government announced that it was considering plans for a more elaborate defence of the estuary, a 10-mile-long barrier, stretching from Sheerness across to Southend. The good news – the scheme would effectively seal off the entire entrance to the Thames in the event of a surge tide. The bad news – watch out Thanet.

ENGINEERING DISASTERS

WOULD HE HAVE BEEN THE FIRST MAN TO FLY AN AEROPLANE?

■ *A tragic death on 2 October 1899 robbed the county – and the country – of its most promising chance to become the first site for heavier-than-air manned flight. But for that day's fatal twist of fate, the Wright brothers might easily have been 'also flowns' and the name (unlikely though it may sound) on everyone's lips would have been one Percy Sinclair Pilcher.*

PILCHER IS ONE OF OUR least celebrated technical wizards, the father of flying in Britain, who conducted most of his experiments in the tranquil valley of Eynsford, south of Swanley. He had been a lecturer in naval architecture and marine engineering at Glasgow University since 1891, but he left what would have been a steady career for his real love, experimenting with flying machines.

He initially came to Kent to work for the eccentric American inventor Hiram Maxim who was also an early experimenter in manned flight, building a cumbersome and highly unlikely steam-powered craft at his country estate near Dartford. Pilcher soon broke away, found the idyllic retreat of Eynsford and began building his machine, *The Hawk*, essentially a hang-glider in today's terms, with a wingspan of over 23 ft, yet weighing less than 50 lbs.

Beginning in 1896, he made a series of gliding experiments along the Darent valley at Upper Austin Lodge farm, just south of Eynsford village – the first manned aircraft flights in Britain. He used the steep

PERCY PILCHER – KENT'S FORGOTTEN AVIATION PIONEER. HE WOULD ALMOST CERTAINLY HAVE BEATEN THE WRIGHT BROTHERS BUT FOR HIS UNTIMELY DEATH.

sides of the valley to launch himself off down one side and he rose to anything up to 40 ft above the ground for distances of up to 300 ft. He built an elaborate launching device much like a catapult to give him extra impetus.

While a successful pioneer of gliding, he always recognised that his endeavours were simply precursors to the real dream – of sustained, powered flight – and he early on envisioned a machine powered by an engine working a screw propeller which would allow flight 'with comparative safety'. In 1896 he set out his ideas in his extraordinary Patent 9144, which is considered by aviation historians to be the world's first practical design for a powered aircraft.

In June 1897, his *Hawk* glided more than 750 yards, then a record for a heavier-than-air machine. This was fully three years before the Wrights had even entered the flight business. At the time they were still bicycle makers who had not even begun to consider experimenting with flying at all.

Pilcher then set to work to design an engine that was both light enough and powerful enough for the job. By the summer of 1899 – just at the time that the Wrights had decided to start experimenting with gliders – he had patented an engine that generated 4 hp but weighed only 40 lbs, and had an engineer starting to build it. So tantalisingly close, fate then intervened.

Always anxious to demonstrate his machines to anyone who would take an interest, Pilcher accepted an invitation from a distinguished

THE MEMORIAL AT STAMFORD HALL, LEICESTERSHIRE, ON THE SPOT WHERE PILCHER CRASHED ON SEPTEMBER 30, 1899. (COURTESY OF MAT FASCIONE, WWW.GEOGRAPH.ORG.UK/PHOTO/592910 – USED UNDER LICENCE).

friend, Lord Braye, to demonstrate his glider at the peer's Leicestershire home. In the grounds at Market Harborough on Saturday, 30 September, he was flying at 30 ft when a small rod in the tail of his craft broke and he crashed, severely injuring himself. He lingered for two days. When he died on the Monday he was aged just 32.

History's accolade for inventing powered, sustained and controlled heavier-than-air flight would go elsewhere. But for Pilcher's infectious wish to share his dreams with others, it would almost certainly have been very different and it would have been the Eynsford Hawk, not Kitty Hawk, the site of the Wrights' first powered flight in North Carolina, that would occupy premier place in the annals of aviation.

THE FIRST PARACHUTE DEATH

■ *A new aeronautical device was tested at Greenwich, then very much a part of the county of Kent, in the summer of 1837 with, what the newspapers of the time called, 'melancholy' results, bringing about the first known parachute fatality in history.*

Robert Cocking, a pioneer of parachuting, was experimenting with his latest model and went ahead with a demonstration in July 1837 in the teeth of persistent warnings by his close friends that the structure was unsafe, unaerodynamic and destined – rightly it turned out – for disaster.

It was the most curious-looking contraption, best described as an inverted cone, 34 ft in diameter at the top and coming down to just 3 or 4 ft at the bottom, with a round, open hole. A structure less conducive to steady descent it would be difficult to design. A close colleague, a Mr Green, urged him the night before the trial, and during most of the following morning, to give up the attempt, actually showing him calculations he had done and double-checked with other scientists, which doubted the wisdom of the enterprise.

Cocking was unrepentant, maintaining that his chute could bear 120 lbs more stress than would be required. He instructed the preparations to proceed and in the early afternoon on 24 July, Green and another assistant, Mr Spencer, fired up a mother balloon, attached to which was Cocking's contraption with him in another basket underneath, and the three men lifted off.

At 5,000 ft Cocking cut the ties with the balloon and descended – with violent abandon. The parachute fell into a field just over a mile away near Lee about 70 seconds later. Crowds were quickly on the scene to find Cocking in a heap, thrown out of his basket by the impact and, with a frightfully gashed head, close to death. From the crushed corners of the basket, it was pretty clear that he had crashed into the ground at an alarming speed. He died within minutes.

His colleagues, still aloft, were oblivious to the tragedy. They sailed on and came down twenty miles further on at Offham, near Malling, about nine in the evening, staying the night there. News of their friend's death only caught up with them the following morning. By that time, Cocking's body and the remains of the parachute had been taken to the Tiger's Head pub at Lee. Fevered interest quickly led to the landlord being asked for viewings. Seeing a good opportunity for profit, he began selling tickets. The parachute could be viewed at sixpence a head and Cocking's body could be seen for another sixpence.

Also quickly out of the woodwork was the 'I told you so' brigade. While it was not clear whether the cone-shaped structure had collapsed in flight or only when it hit the ground, commentators rushed to publish their calculations proving the flight was doomed from the beginning. One, perhaps reasonably, casting mockery on the demerits of the cone as opposed to the flat parachute, estimated that Cocking's construction had five times too little chute for the weight he exerted.

The inquest opened two days later and concluded on the 28th with a verdict that he met his death accidentally (quaintly, in those days termed 'casually', which his death was anything but). Furthermore, the relatives of the unfortunate Cocking were not permitted to get the parachute back. Under the legal custom of the time any moving object that caused the death of a person was curiously declared 'deodand' (literally, 'thing to be given to God') and forfeited to the Crown for charitable purposes. As the parachute was most definitely moving, the new queen, who had ascended the throne only the previous month, got her most unexpected and least useful accession present of all.

THE FIRST SAFETY PRECAUTIONS FOR THE GOODWIN SANDS

■ *For centuries, the Goodwins have been the cause of disaster and tragedy in our neck of the woods.*

In November 1954, the Goodwin Sands claimed their most ironic victim – the lightship moored there to prevent other ships from going aground. This came about during what accounts of the tragedy called the worst gale in living memory. The *South Goodwin* broke her

THE MOST IRONIC VICTIM OF THE GOODWIN SANDS
– ITS OWN LIGHTSHIP, NOVEMBER 1954.

moorings and was driven up the eastern side of the Sands and capsized, drowning all seven of the crew. Only one person, a visiting scientist, survived. At first light the next day, rescuers found her lying abjectly on her side on the exposed bank, already half-buried in sand.

Tragic though it was, it was just another small entry in the mind-boggling catalogue of disaster that stretches back over centuries. The Sands have acquired a lore all of their own and produced some bizarre chapters in the annals of the county. Just eleven miles long, they have accounted for well over a thousand documented sinkings in the past four hundred years. Countless other vessels have disappeared without trace. In the heyday of sailing traffic – between the 1830s and the 1870s – losses were astoundingly frequent. For the last two decades of that period they averaged almost two a month.

The Sands provoked curious practices on land too – landlords divided up the coast between themselves to claim rights over vessels which foundered on their 'patch' but most often the sight of a ship in trouble on the Sands prompted a manic free-for-all amongst coastal dwellers who raced out in little boats to help themselves to the cargo, as they were then entitled to do if the ship had been abandoned.

The presence of any living soul – even a dog as in one 17th-century instance – meant that the ship became a derelict rather than a wreck and preserved the owner's rights, a fine legal point that was rarely allowed to hinder the scavenging packs who descended on a ship, very often despatching any remaining crew or passengers in the process.

Everything was fair game. Perhaps the strangest affair of the kind was the fate of the cargo ship *Earl of Eglinton*, which foundered in January 1860, chiefly, it emerged afterwards, because the captain refused to agree terms with the pilot sent out to guide her through the Sands. As was customary when the authorities got control, the salvaged cargo was sold off at public auction the following week. The curiosity though was that even some of the ship's timber was salvaged, sufficient to build a three-storey house which stood for over eighty years at St Margaret's Bay, appropriately christened Eglinton Cottage. It perished in 1940, a victim of a Second World War bomb. The *Eglinton*'s bell still hangs nearby, in St Andrew's church, Buckland in Dover as a more permanent memorial.

The Goodwins were perhaps a little safer for the maritime traveller in September 1840, following the opening of the first-ever safety device to be erected on the Sands themselves. The strange contraption was the brainchild of one Captain Bullock and amounted to a 'do-it-yourself' survival kit.

Bullock's invention consisted of a 40 ft wooden mast with a gallery, which could hold up to forty people towards the top. When a ship foundered on the sandbanks, victims could make their way at low tide across to it, climb a chain ladder and find refuge in the gallery. From the masthead, they would fly a blue flag that could be seen by the authorities on the shore to summon help.

The gallery was (comparatively) sumptuous. A small supply of bread, water and spirits was always available, and around the sides of the gallery sailcloth sheets could be unrolled and fastened enclosing the whole gallery like a tent. There was even a basket chair fixed to a pulley system to lift anyone who could not climb the ladder. Instructions were written in eight languages around the gallery – simple and to the point: 'Hoist the Flag.'

Observers at the time ridiculed Bullock's idea that anything substantial could be secured on the shifting sands of the Goodwins. It was true that his 'refuge beacon' was fixed by piling several tons of ballast around the cross-shaped oak feet and by the eight iron chains to which the tower was tethered. Still, the beauty of the idea in Bullock's eyes was that it was disposable. To those who objected that there was 'nothing in the mode of construction which holds out a premise of perpetuity', as one contemporary wrote, he answered that it could be replaced at 'trifling expense'.

The opening ceremony on 10 September 1840 was conducted by Bullock himself, along with Captain Boys, the Superintendent of the Deal Naval Storeyard. Boys' first action was to scale the mast and fly a Union Jack from the masthead.

Against expectations, the unlikely construction survived for four years. It handled most storms but ironically could not deal with human intervention.

In August 1844 it was run down by what a contemporary account called the 'reprehensible carelessness' of a passing Dutch ship. Bullock rebuilt it and it was back to working order within two months, this time with an iron mast and ten times the amount of ballast. It stood for a further three years but in December 1847 Trinity House, the official body responsible for coastal navigation, issued a memo to shipowners stating, simply and without further explanation, that it had 'disappeared'.

BUILDING A HOUSE ON SAND: THE MISPLACED GOODWIN SANDS LIGHTHOUSE

■ *The early attempts to build a refuge beacon were not the only ideas around for improving the safety of mariners navigating the Goodwins. William Bush, an inventive obsessive, submitted plans at the same time as Captain Bullock's (see previous entry) for putting up a permanent lighthouse. His ideas were so advanced for the time that it would take four attempts to bring them to fruition, only for*

*him to discover that he had built it in the wrong place. His dream
was one long nightmare.*

William Bush's plans envisaged a more ambitious endeavour than a
mere safety refuge. The eccentric Deptford engineer aimed to build
the first lighthouse on the Sands themselves.

His design was fiendishly clever. It comprised a huge iron tube with
a flattened out bottom, much like an upturned ice cream cone. His
scheme was to plant the cone on the Sands and then from the inside
dig out the foundations, allowing the cone to sink ever deeper into its
sand foundations. The lighthouse would be formed by adding
sections to the top. In theory, as the contraption became heavier, the
deeper it would sink by force of its own weight into the sand and
hence become more firmly grounded.

He built his iron cone in the naval yard at Deal. The huge piece was
ready to be towed out in October 1841. Then the first of the disasters
that were to plague Bush's project occurred. Ironically for an
enterprise of this purpose, the ship towing it out to the Goodwins ran
aground on the Sands. The cone broke away, had to be retrieved, and
was towed back to Deal harbour where it promptly sank. It was too
large to salvage in one piece, so Bush had to watch as it was cut up,
taken back to the yard and put back together again.

It was July the following year before Bush was ready for the second
attempt. On the 28th, the cone made landfall on the Sands after a
seven-hour operation. However, matters were still not straightforward
– literally. The cone settled into the sand at an unsightly 1 in 12 lean.
Work began on the foundations and by September Bush had sunk the
cone 25 ft down and corrected the lean. He thought he had hit solid
chalk and was content. (It was many years later that the actual depth
to rock was discovered to be over 75 ft.)

Convinced he had a solid base, he then began adding the iron rings
to the top of the cone to form the body of the lighthouse.
Unfortunately, just when everything looked to be going smoothly, a
storm in October blew a passing ship into the structure, knocking the
entire edifice horizontal.

Again undaunted, Bush rebuilt it all during 1843, only for it to be destroyed in another storm early in the following year. With his fourth effort to rebuild, Bush took no chances. The basement was filled with 400 tons of stone, concrete and cement. Nothing was going to shift it. To mark the opening ceremony on 19 January 1845, he held a party on the viewing platform and hosted his guests to a dinner of roast beef and plum pudding.

Bush actually camped out on the structure for most of the first six months of 1845, experimenting to see how deep the Sands in fact were. His wife and child joined him for a fortnight. This is thought to be the only record of a home being established on the Goodwins.

Bush's five years of overcoming setback after setback all came to nothing, however, due to one bizarre oversight. Consumed to distraction by the technical challenges he constantly had to overcome, Bush had forgotten to take care of one small matter. He had ended up building his lighthouse in entirely the wrong place.

It was four-square in the middle of the Sands, and Trinity House, the government authority in charge of coastal safety, told him that when working as a lighthouse it would actually serve as a dangerous invitation to shipping to come much closer to the sandbank than was safe. They instructed him to take it all down, something they reminded him they had been telling him to do for six months before he had ignored them and opened it.

He reluctantly complied – £12,000 down on the whole exercise (about half a million pounds in today's values). However, the foundations were too well entrenched and could not be removed; they remain there to this day.

A DISASTROUS TESTING OF A NEW WEAPON OF WAR

■ *One of the world's earliest experiments with a new devilish weapon of war took place on 1 September 1858, at the normally peaceful resort of Herne Bay. Captain John Harvey, pioneer inventor, had announced the public trial of his revolutionary device – the torpedo. It was a far cry from today's self-propelled, self-guided missile, but the impact of the day's events on the residents of the Kent seaside town were long remembered.*

Harvey had built prototypes of the torpedo some years earlier and they had been used by the Russian navy in its fight with Turkey in 1854 before that scrap escalated into the Crimean War. The results had not been particularly encouraging. Of the four sent against the Turkish fleet, three hadn't found their target at all while the fourth did manage to hit something but failed to explode.

The detonation of these early devices was a touch-and-go affair, relying on a glass ampoule of acid breaking on impact to mix with chemicals that would cause a flame which set light to a fuse which ultimately detonated – or not, if any of these steps failed. The other drawback was that they were not self-propelled – it would be another decade before engines were fitted. These pioneering versions were dragged behind a ship with a holding device that set the torpedo out to one side of the mother ship. The ship then had to manoeuvre up to the enemy and try to land the device against it – rather like a remote controlled mine. It was hardly the most inconspicuous way to attack.

Harvey was staying near Herne Bay and in the late summer of 1858 had reached the moment for another trial. He obtained from the coastguards a derelict ship, which he moored off the seafront. Crowds gathered on the appointed day to see the spectacle, but for several hours and several runs of Harvey's control boat the experimenters failed to connect.

Giving it all up as a bad job, a despondent Harvey returned to shore and had retired to his carriage to go home. His aides were packing up and a lone fisherman had the task of reeling in the wooden-cased beast. He perhaps had every reason to presume that he was working with a dud device. But Sod's Law intervened. When the torpedo touched the beach, it unexpectedly detonated. The explosion caused panic on the promenade and devastated all the shop windows on the seafront. The most dramatic impact was on the prominent 80-ft clock tower: all four glass faces were blown to smithereens. It seems the fisherman escaped unhurt for *The Times* reported 'no serious injury to life or limb resulted'.

THE DEFENCE THAT WAS NEVER NEEDED

■ *On 26 September 1804, Prime Minister William Pitt gave the go-ahead for what became Kent's great white elephant – the Royal Military Canal, one of the only two canals ever built in the county (the other was the short-lived Higham–Strood tunnel). It was conceived not with any commercial objectives in mind but as a military defensive cordon skirting the most likely landing site for French invasion: Romney Marsh. By the time it was finished though, the invasion scare was over and the canal started life instantly obsolete.*

The scheme was dreamt up during a frantic period of invasion threats from Napoleon after the resumption of war between the two countries in May 1803 and when every port from the tip of Brittany to Holland was constructing the flat-bottomed barges with which Napoleon planned to invade.

A thousand had been gathered at Boulogne by the end of 1803, sparking panic across the Channel. Romney was always the most obvious site, with its long stretches of low, flat beaches ideal for rapid and unmolested landings. Defensive plans, so far as they existed, were crude in the extreme. At the first sight of an invasion, the entire marsh, which lies below the level of normal high tides, would simply be flooded by opening the sluices in the sea wall at Dymchurch. The shortcomings of the strategy were obvious in hindsight but never considered at the time: flooding would simply have allowed the invading barges to sail further inland!

The idea of a canal came from a military engineer, Lt Col John Brown, who suggested cutting a waterway 60 ft wide and 9 ft deep around the inland perimeter of the marshes, from Hythe in the east to Cliff End, beyond Winchelsea, in the west, a curious ribbon of water effectively sealing off the marshes from the rest of the country. And efficiently too: the projecting nub-shaped coastline – the Dungeness bulge – meant that the 28-mile-long canal encompassed and protected almost double the length of shoreline.

The advance of Napoleon's troops would be forestalled by blowing up the 19 wooden bridges that would span the canal at intervals along its length. The canal would also allow army contingents to be brought rapidly along the canal to wherever they were needed in the battle.

The first cutting was made at Hythe at the end of October 1804 and just twenty-two months later the main stretch had been completed, to Iden where it joined the Rother river for a short length. A further arm from Rye through Winchelsea to Cliff End to complete the seal was finished by September 1808. The project came within budget – a remarkable achievement in itself – at £234,000 (about £6½ million in today's values), but three years after, Napoleon had abandoned his plans to invade and gone off into central Europe on his way to invade Russia.

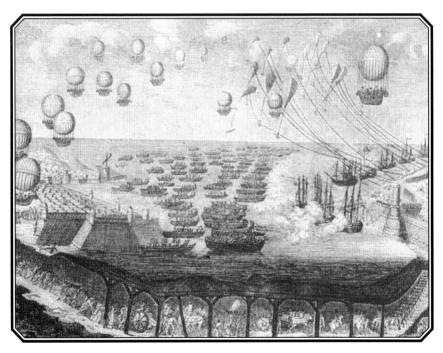

INVASION FROM THE CONTINENT HAS BEEN A PERPETUAL NIGHTMARE.
THIS APOCALYPTIC IMAGE FROM 1805 ENVISAGES NAPOLEON COMING
BY SEA, AIR AND TUNNEL. NOTE THE INGENIOUS AIRBORNE
DEFENCE – MANNED, KITE-BORN MARKSMEN.

Although expenditure was cut to a minimum and many of the extra defensive buildings were never built, maintenance still presented the government with a fearful liability. It was one it bore for seventy years. Efforts to encourage commercial traffic, and through it recoup money from tolls, produced steady but modest returns of £1,000 a year – just about enough to cover basic repairs.

The canal was never a commercial success. Desperate to get it off the government's books, Parliament passed an Act in 1872 permitting the Secretary of State for War to give it away to anyone who would take it. Five years later, the Lords of Romney Marsh agreed to lease most of it for 999 years at an annual rent of just one shilling. Hythe leased its local stretch for £48 a year and Winchelsea's arm was sold off to a private buyer. Since 1909 only pleasure boats have used the waterway.

Would it ever have succeeded if it had been put to the test? It is probably doubtful. The grand scheme had its critics even at the time. Daniel Defoe, when he first saw it, mocked it contemptuously: 'As if those great armies which had crossed the Rhine and the Danube would be deterred by sixty feet of water.'

CATASTROPHIC CHARACTERS

THE RUSSIANS ARE COMING!

■ *Between January and May 1698, Tsar Peter the Great of Russia undertook possibly the most anarchic state visit ever to have descended upon Britain. It was part of his 'Great Embassy', his celebrated grand tour of Europe, which lasted a year and a half and encompassed virtually every centre of civilisation the continent had to offer.*

He and his substantial entourage were given lodgings in Sayes Court, in Deptford, then very much part of Kent. The house was the pride and joy of diarist John Evelyn. Events caused him to deeply regret his generosity in making the loan. It is, though, fortunate for us as he recorded the details of what followed.

Historians still argue whether civilisation ultimately rubbed off on Peter. What was certain was that he clearly brought precious little of it with him.

HEIR TO THE SPIRIT of Ivan the Terrible, Tsar Peter's party hit London like a whirlwind. His purpose was, in one tour, to garner all the secrets of modern technological advances to turn his backward, peasant Russia into a great power. It was the first peaceful contact the rest of Europe had had with Russia since Ivan's fearsome forays into Poland and the Baltic a century and a half before.

Peter came to Britain from Holland where he had spent four months disguised as a Dutch labourer working in the shipyards learning the secrets of modern shipbuilding. He had also visited

PETER THE GREAT. THE REGAL
SPLENDOUR OF HIS OFFICIAL
PORTRAIT BELIES THE CHAOS OF
HIS INNER CHARACTER.

Brussels, where he left a memento illustrating his less regal side – a plaque in the royal park marks the spot where he stopped to be violently sick after one of his many spectacular drinking bouts.

Whether we knew exactly what we were letting ourselves in for is uncertain. His arrival on 11 January 1698 via a sedate royal procession up the Thames gave no indication of the mayhem to come. After a warm formal welcome from William III, Peter launched on a hectic tour of workshops and factories, amassing technical specifications by the cartload. He was particularly enamoured by the Royal Observatory at Greenwich and imposed himself on the Astronomer Royal, John Flamsteed, on four occasions.

The house Peter had been loaned – Sayes Court – was in the then countrified Deptford suburb. It was chosen since it lay conveniently near the dockyard. John Evelyn had spent 45 years painstakingly laying out the gardens, perfecting a bowling green, designing pathways and ornamental attractions. It was quite literally a house fit for a king – but, unfortunately as it turned out, not a king like Peter.

In the four months of the visit, the Tsar and his entourage wrecked the lot. Evelyn got anxious warnings of the destruction being wreaked but the true calamity only became apparent when he returned there after Peter's departure. He called Sir Christopher Wren in to draw up an inventory and an estimate of the cost. Wren found the floors and carpets so stained and smeared with ink and grease that the whole

THE STUDIED ORDER OF DEPTFORD'S MEMORIAL COMMEMORATING
PETER THE GREAT'S VISIT BELIES THE CHAOS HE LEFT BEHIND.

house had to be re-floored. Tiles had been prised off walls and door locks pulled apart, no doubt all in the cause of investigation. All the paintwork was filthy dirty and over 300 glass windowpanes were broken. Every chair in the house – and there had been over fifty – had simply disappeared, probably into the stove. Feather quilts and sheets were ripped and over twenty paintings were torn – the evidence suggested that they had been used for target practice.

Outside the carnage was impressive. The lawn had been turned into mud 'as if regiments of soldiers in iron shoes had drilled on it'. The magnificent hedge, stretching in its full glory 400 ft in length, 9 ft high and 5 ft thick, had been flattened – by having wheelbarrows rammed through it. It seems that the Russians had found some wheelbarrows, which were unheard of back home, and had devised an entertaining sport consisting of one man, usually the Tsar, sitting in one and having an aide career him through the gardens.

Wren's estimate came to £350 and ninepence, a sum which sounds inconsequential but equates to something in the order of £20,000 in today's values, which the government hastily coughed up to prevent any undesirable publicity.

Peter's departure was a rather more sedate affair. He left the steps at Whitehall on 2 May. Sailing his yacht *Royal Transport*, a gift from William, he put into Woolwich in the afternoon for a final tour of the dockyard and to say farewell to those at the arsenal with whom he had become a familiar visitor. By dusk he had reached Gravesend where he moored for the night. On 3 May, he made for Chatham and spent most of the day there, sailing round the harbour and once again visiting the dockyard. The following day, the county finally got shot of him as he reached Margate where he picked up his English naval escort for the journey back across the North Sea. A heavy sigh of relief must have greeted the news that he had gone. He didn't get a second invitation.

Sayes Court had an even less auspicious future. It was almost all demolished in 1728 and what was left was converted into a workhouse. Part of the grounds became a public park in 1877. Even today, however, there are reminders of that momentous visit. On the site there is a Sayes Court, a Sayes Court Street and a Czar Street all running off the main A200 which at this point is called Evelyn Street.

FAVERSHAM'S DISASTROUS ROYAL RELIC

■ *Stephen was one of England's weakest, and most disastrous, kings. He is one of only two monarchs to be buried in Kent. He died on 25 October 1154 at Dover Castle after an acute attack of appendicitis aggravated by bleeding piles. By all accounts he was in great agony. The contemporary chroniclers agree that it was a most fitting end to a reign in which the king had loosed anarchy on the country and inflicted almost continuous civil war.*

So unstable was his time, Stephen is the only king to have had himself crowned three times to emphasise his authority. He owed his place on the throne to curious circumstances. He was, in fact, French and, together with his wife, owned vast estates along the French coast. He was the nephew of the English King Henry I, who died in 1135 without a legitimate (i.e. male) heir. Henry had struck a deal with some of the English barons to recognise his daughter, Matilda, as Queen of England. That fell apart upon his death. It is likely that a faction of the barons, unwilling to accept a woman in charge of them, and sensing a possible 'pawn' in Stephen, encouraged him to come over and take the throne. His proximity to the English coast meant he could also arrive quickly after Henry's death. So, he landed in Kent, sped to London and claimed the crown.

He was crowned for the first time on St Stephen's Day, 26 December 1135. His first act was to hurry down to the old royal capital at Winchester and seize the state treasury, some £100,000 worth of jewels, gold and cash, which he began feverishly distributing to the barons as a friendly gesture that would encourage them to continue supporting his position. When it was safe for his wife to join him, he held a second coronation ceremony the following March when she formally became queen and Stephen reasserted his own status by a repeat crowning of himself.

There followed nearly twenty years of instability throughout the country in which the king's authority was constantly challenged. Personally a weak character, he inspired rebellion from Welsh and Scottish hordes and from factions of his barons. The presence of a rival claimant to the throne guaranteed turmoil. Matilda, who had been carefully watching developments from France, finally invaded in 1139 and spent two years battling for the crown in a vicious civil war. She managed to capture Stephen at a battle in Lincoln and declared she would keep him a prisoner for life.

Stephen's wife, confusingly another Matilda – Matilda of Boulogne – then took over the royal armies and, in the middle of the battle of the Matildas, managed to beat the claimant for control of London and capture claimant Matilda's brother whom she held in order to bargain for Stephen. The king was released in an exchange in November 1141 after almost a year of imprisonment and to celebrate the restoration of his control, he had yet another coronation – this time at Canterbury Cathedral – on Christmas Day 1141.

EVEN OFFICIAL PORTRAITS OF
KING STEPHEN SEEM TO CONVEY
A LESS THAN ENDEARING
PERSONALITY.

The civil war continued for another seven years and the country descended into more anarchy – barons building castles which they used to terrorise the countryside around; no man's cattle were safe, it was said, and the concept of 'robber barons' came into existence. For probably the only time in its history, famine stalked the English countryside as crops rotted in the fields or were stolen.

Stephen spent most of his last year, 1154, in Kent, which had remained loyal to him throughout. The chroniclers called Stephen's nineteen-year reign 'nineteen long winters' and when 'Christ and his saints were asleep'. So no one mourned his passing. He was buried in his favourite place, Faversham Abbey, which he and his wife had founded. She had died three years earlier and was already interred there along with his son and only heir, who had died within the past year. So, without a son to succeed him, it fell to his rival Matilda's son to rule as Henry II.

Nothing of the tomb survives today. A traditional story has it that during the destruction of the monasteries in Henry VIII's time, Stephen's coffin was stolen for its lead and his bones thrown into Faversham Creek. It is probable that his wife and their son suffered the same fate.

For the record, the other monarch buried in Kent is the 15th-century King Henry IV, who lies in Canterbury Cathedral.

THE TOWN THAT DIDN'T READ THE SCRIPT

■ *The inhabitants of Faversham achieved a day of infamy in 1688 when they managed the curious feat of ending up in the bad books of both opposing sides in the 'Glorious Revolution', which saw the toppling of Catholic James II in favour of the Protestant Dutch sovereign William, Prince of Orange.*

The intricacies of the plotting that contrived to force James out need not concern us, but it all came to a head in the early hours of 11 December 1688 when James, still legally king, decided he had had enough and arranged to be spirited away from his palace in London, with the aim of fleeing into exile on the Continent. What followed was a comedy of errors approaching a farce. The king's disappearance suited everyone involved in organising a smooth transfer of the monarchy, but no one had reckoned with the piratical urges of some coastal Kent fishermen.

James' chief assistant in his escape was the head of an ancient Kentish family, Sir Edward Hales, who held estates around Tenterden and had recently also bought Hackington, near Canterbury. Hales was a stout Jacobean and he arranged the details of James' flight.

Dressed as Hales' servant, the king was taken across the Thames at Vauxhall where a carriage awaited to bring him out of London and through the county to a rendezvous with a fishing boat in the Swale at Elmley Island. Hales and the king reached the coast in the early evening as the crew on the escape vessel were making final preparations. A stormy passage was forecast late in the day, with bad weather said to be likely in the North Sea, so the crew decided to load on more ballast.

The extra time and the sight of not a few rather well-dressed courtiers agitating heatedly for a rapid departure only served to attract attention to the party. At eleven o'clock at night, just as they were on the point of leaving, three boatloads of fishermen from Faversham who had heard of the unusual happenings arrived in the river and boarded the boat.

It was intended to be a purely mercenary exercise – noblemen fleeing with all their wealth were easy pickings. As a local notable, Hales was recognised immediately, but James was mistaken for a notorious Jesuit priest who was known to be on the run (so even his capture at all was in fact a pure accident). The troupe were marshalled together and instructed to leave the boat and go ashore.

James was by all accounts roughly handled and his money and valuables stolen although the fishermen missed the coronation rings and they thought the diamonds in his jewel-encrusted buckle were glass. Nevertheless, their haul amounted to 300 guineas and a pair of gold medals.

The fishermen landed their catch at Faversham and conveyed them to the Queen's Arms in the town. It was there that one of the civic leaders recognised the 'priest' for who he really was and announced to the flabbergasted fishermen that they had in fact taken their king prisoner.

As it became clear that a royal flight had been stopped in its tracks, the folk of Faversham, still a little overawed, began to congratulate themselves on their perspicacity. James was lodged in the mayor's house and exultant messages sent off to London to alert the council of peers, the provisional government. While James pleaded for his life by haranguing the crowd that William of Orange's arrival would mean the execution of another English king and that Faversham would have to take its place in history as the town which yielded the monarch up to the regicides, the government in London received the news with a dismay bordering on anger.

The news of the shabby handling of the king had sparked a surge of sympathy for James and the last thing those trying to manoeuvre the transition of the crown wanted was a public scene. In fact, the council would have preferred it if James had left the country quietly and unhindered. That would have been the end of the matter. Instead, they had a monarch locked up amid a feverish atmosphere in Faversham and the stirrings of Catholic sympathy in the capital. They were not best pleased with the fishermen of Faversham.

A troop of lifeguards descended on the town to rescue the king and for the second time in as many days, the townsfolk felt the wrath of authority. They could be forgiven for feeling a bit confused and disillusioned by it all and an air of fearfulness about repercussions settled on the town.

James was removed to Rochester to allow the authorities time to decide what to do. They eventually concluded that they did not want James back in London in the present climate and sent a message telling his captors to keep him at Rochester. Unfortunately by the time the message got through, James had already been allowed to go on his way back to the capital.

When he arrived in London, he was promptly given a state banquet to try to make up for his discomforts and then despatched downriver back to Rochester – on a royal barge guarded this time by a platoon of Dutch soldiers. That was on 18 December. The arrangements for guarding him at Rochester were deliberately lax, almost as if he was to be encouraged to try to escape again.

Four days later he did, in the middle of the night, slipping away on a barge to Shellness at the eastern end of the Isle of Sheppey where a French vessel took him away. All in London breathed a heavy sigh of relief. The obstacle to a peaceful succession was gone.

James never forgot the rude treatment he received at the hands of his Faversham captors. Four years later when he announced an 'amnesty' for those who had conspired against him when still the legitimate king of the day, it was accompanied by a long list of explicit exceptions, and prominent amongst them were the fishermen of Faversham.

KENT'S MOST NOTORIOUS ASSASSINATION

■ *Kent's most famous crime, the killing of Archbishop Thomas Becket, took place on the steps of the altar in Canterbury Cathedral around five o'clock on the evening of 29 December 1170. It was not exactly the stealthy ambush in the dark affair that is often portrayed.*

The four knights who carried out the deed had, earlier in the afternoon, heatedly confronted Becket in the Archbishop's Palace in front of a whole retinue of monks. They had then left and Becket carried on his normal business preparing for the evening service. The monks, fearing an attack at any time, urged him to hide himself away but he refused, insisting on making the regular procession from the Palace through the grounds to the cathedral.

The monks, whom the chroniclers describe as being scared to death, had to accompany him as usual. A picturesque image is left by one historian: 'The whole march was a struggle between the obstinate attempt of the Primate to preserve his dignity and the frantic eagerness of his attendants to gain the sanctuary.'

Becket had to protest to his monks about being dragged hurriedly to the cathedral. He ordered them not to secure the doors and ensured they were open. All but one of the monks fled, secreting themselves in nooks and crannies of the cathedral. Watched and heard by them, Becket met his fate, struck with blows so heavy that one of the killers' swords shattered in two as it hit the floor.

Becket's quarrel with Henry II had lasted eight years, the last six of which he had spent in exile in France. It turned on the age-old question of who – king or pope – had final authority in England (a dispute not eventually settled until four centuries later by Henry VIII).

Becket had left the country in 1164, only two years after becoming archbishop, after boldly telling the king to his face that only the pope could pronounce punishment on him. From the physical safety of France, Becket carried on his campaign and the pair hurled insults at each other by a constant exchange of letters. The two appeared to have reached an impasse.

It would be Henry's act in getting Becket's ecclesiastical rival the Archbishop of York to preside over a coronation ceremony in June 1170, declaring the king's son formally the heir to the throne, that really irked Becket. If there was one thing worse than being insulted it was being ignored. He lost no time getting the pope to excommunicate the archbishop and he rushed back to England with the letters of expulsion and had arrived at the beginning of December. His return and excommunication of the Archbishop of York had prompted Henry's celebrated outburst about ridding him of turbulent priests – taken by the knights as their cue.

Becket had told several people before leaving France that he was convinced he would not outlive the year. On the fateful day itself, his first words in the morning to his personal attendant were to ask whether there was any possibility of escaping the city before daybreak. When they answered that there was, he told them they should do so. He had his usual banquet at three o'clock in the afternoon, before the killers arrived, and was seen to drink more than usual. His cup bearer remarked on this to him and Becket replied 'He who has much blood to shed must drink much.'

The day of Becket's death was a Tuesday. Historians have pointed to the curious coincidence that almost every significant event in Becket's life happened on a Tuesday. He was born (and baptised on the same day) on a Tuesday, 21 December 1118. It was on a Tuesday that he left the country in 1164 after his showdown with the king. It was on a Tuesday, shortly before he returned, that he had his premonition that he would be killed. He returned to England on a Tuesday (1 December 1170). It would also be on a Tuesday that Becket's great antagonist, the king, would be buried, and on a Tuesday that the grand ceremony re-interring his remains in the famous Becket shrine took place in 1220. But then all of this is rather appropriate since, according to the old doggerel, Tuesday's child ... is full of grace.

THE EXTREME HUNTSMAN

On 6 August 1822, it was finally safe for God's creatures to go back into the countryside around Canterbury when the manic shooting squire of Littlebourne started out on his journey to meet his maker. His hunting career is probably unparalleled – at least in the detail with which the perpetrator recorded his 'sporting' achievements.

Henry Denne, landowner and Lord of the Manor of Littlebourne, a few miles east of Canterbury, was one of the best marksmen of his day and took great pride in recording his feats for the presumed adulation of posterity. Between 1770 and 1809, after which he either became too old to shoot or his rapacious rate declined to such an embarrassing extent that he stopped counting, he kept meticulous records of every single animal he shot on his estate, and quite a slaughter it was: 3,764 rabbits, 2,552 snipe, 2,322 partridges, 2,079 hares, 1,682 woodcock, 753 pheasants, 700 landrail, 600 wildfowl and 2 eagles, a total of almost fourteen and a half thousand animals, or one every single day of the nearly forty years he kept counting.

He was clearly very proud of his lifetime's work. In his will, he asked for a permanent testimonial to it. He stipulated that his tomb should be inscribed with carvings of all the animals he had shot – rather like a latter day fighter pilot adorning his aircraft with emblems for his kills. The local church tastefully refused him his last wish, allowing him just the two eagles that now surmount the huge granite block standing in the town's churchyard.

Rather appropriately, in modern times occupants of the same land are giving something in return. Just a mile or so from the churchyard, part of the old estate is now home to one of Kent's largest zoo parks.

THE LAST BRITISH SOLDIER TO FALL IN ACTION ON ENGLISH SOIL

■ *A quiet corner of Kent secured for itself a place in the nation's history by being the location for what is believed to be the last occasion a soldier of the British army died in a ground action on English soil.*

The incident – bizarre in itself – occurred on 31 May 1838, near the village of Dunkirk, just west of Canterbury. A platoon of the 45th regiment stationed at Canterbury were called out to enforce a warrant issued by magistrates for the arrest of 'Sir' William Courtenay, self-styled Messiah who had established a commune of followers in Bossenden Wood at Dunkirk.

Courtenay had been a thorn in the side of the Establishment for a number of years. An ordinary Cornishman, plain John Tom from Truro by birth, he awarded himself his new name and title and developed an extravagantly fiery political campaign exploiting the

THIS DEPICTION OF THE BATTLE OF BOSSENDEN WOOD IS SAID TO BE AN
EYEWITNESS ACCOUNT DRAWN FROM A NEWSPAPER OF THE DAY.

distress of the agricultural classes. He came to east Kent as it was the
country's centre for Luddite-type action against agricultural
machinery and rick burning.

He had tried to whip up a following by standing for Parliament six
years before. Of the 9,500 votes cast in the election, 'Sir William' got
just three. Not one to be put off by such minor set backs, he pressed
his campaign by starting a newspaper which preached an incoherent
mix of anti-Establishment views.

His troubles with the law began in 1837 when he was arrested for
fraud. To avoid transportation, he pleaded insanity and was confined
in an asylum for a year. Now just released, he had returned to
Dunkirk and began his inflammatory agitation once more.

Magistrates moved to arrest him again but early on that May
morning a constable sent to take him into custody was shot and
slashed to death by Courtenay. When news of the outrage reached
Canterbury, a troop of soldiers was hastily despatched to seize him.
The showdown came in the woods where Courtenay and an armed
gang of his followers refused to surrender and opened fire. The army

returned a salvo, killing him and nine of his men. The 45th suffered one fatality: Lieutenant Henry Bennett whom, according to the special plaque in Canterbury Cathedral that records the event, 'fell in the strict and manly discharge of his duties', the last serviceman to do so in England.

Dunkirk remembers its infamous resident today too: the main road running out of the village into the woods is called Courtenay Road – but how many know the story behind it?

THE CRAZY MEN IN THEIR FLYING MACHINE

■ *The increasingly farcical exploits of the 'hopping Yank' captured the county's imagination for three weeks in the summer of 1910. John B. Moisant was attempting to be the first airman to fly the Channel carrying a passenger, and the first to reach London.*

Rapidly running out of flying 'firsts' in this part of the world – Blériot had flown across the Channel a year before and the Englishman Charles Rolls (he of Rolls-Royce) had completed the first non-stop double crossing only two months earlier – the American airman John B. Moisant decided that his only chance of entering the aeronautical hall of fame was to try the first trip across with a passenger, and to make for London.

It was only Moisant's fifth flight ever and he took with him his faithful French engineer, Albert Fileux. On a blustery and cold morning at 5.30 just after dawn on 17 August 1910 they set off from Calais. On reaching the English coast, Moisant tried to find Blériot's landing site, believing he was over Dover; he was in fact over Deal. He gave up and came down on Telegraph Farm at Tilmanstone, five miles inland.

The plane was quickly surrounded by bemused sightseers and Moisant eagerly signed autographs. According to one account, it was here that the true purpose of the trip was only now revealed to the poor Fileux, who appeared to be under the impression that the enterprise was a simple trip across to the Kent coast. He was looking forward to a quick trip home. Moisant announced that his destination was the capital, and he would land in Hyde Park. Within the hour they were off on what was to become a comical procession across the county that would last all of three weeks.

Strong headwinds forced them down near Sittingbourne where they crashed into a turnip field and needed two days for poor Fileux to repair the aircraft. On the 20th, up they went again: and down they came shortly thereafter at Upchurch, four miles further on, still short of Gillingham, breaking the propeller in the process.

By now the public were following the events with increased excitement in these daredevil days. The *Daily Mirror* stepped in, anxious to recapture publicity lost to its rival the *Daily Mail* who had put up the prize for Blériot's feat. They rushed a new propeller to Moisant and Fileux. Oddly, Blériot himself had heard of Moisant's accident and had also arranged for a propeller to be sent from France. The mad race of the propellers was won by the *Mirror*, and on Moisant went.

From Upchurch, he crash-landed at Rainham a mile further on, then again at Wrotham after an impressive 12-mile hop and more drastically at Kemsing after another four miles. Another shattered propeller; but again the *Mirror* came to the rescue, retrieving Blériot's gift which had by now arrived at Dover and bringing it up to the stricken American.

By 26 August they were ready for their sixth flight since landing in Britain. They had covered less than 50 miles. They had enjoyed the hospitality of the local squire at Kemsing while repairs were being done and, to show his gratitude, Moisant agreed to the squire's request to circle the house so that his bedridden wife could see an aircraft for the first time in her life. As he did so, he narrowly missed the chimney pots on the roof, lost control and hit a tree. It was to be another ten days before they were able to move again.

On 6 September, the seventh leg of the journey saw the repaired craft successfully take off ... and true to form come down again a couple of miles away between Otford and Shoreham. A quick tinker by the doughty Fileux and they were off, heading for the metropolis.

The authorities there had watched the events unfolding with undisguised alarm. Moisant's increasingly erratic progress towards them sowed rather large doubts in their minds about his ability to

MOISANT, IN PARIS, AT THE START OF HIS JOURNEY.

land safely in the middle of the city. They had told him that he should aim for Crystal Palace, which was several times larger than Hyde Park.

Moisant duly found the open space early in the afternoon, circled the great glass palace but because of haze could not spot the large white arrow that had been laid out on the ground to guide him. He flew off and came down a mile and a quarter away on a piece of land near Beckenham station. He landed heavily and once again wrote off his propeller.

The thousands waiting for him at Crystal Palace were treated to the sight of Moisant's less than triumphal ending to the bizarre trip – both the aviators and their aircraft were hauled by road into the grounds of the park for the reception. It was the safest and most reliable leg of the entire odyssey.

END ODDITIES

A GHOSTLY TRAGEDY REPLAYS ITSELF

■ *Over 250 years ago, the Goodwin Sands claimed one of its strangest and most poignant victims in a tragedy that, it is said, recurs every fifty years on the anniversary in a ghostly recreation.*

THE FATEFUL LAST JOURNEY was that of the *Lady Luvibund* sailing from London to Oporto on 13 February 1748. The ship was owned by Captain Simon Reed, who earlier that day had been married. His young bride, Annetta, was sailing with him. The trip to Portugal was to be a honeymoon and on board that night the newlyweds were holding their reception below decks with Annetta's mother and a gathering of friends.

At the helm the first mate John Rivers was in command. Rivers and Reed were old acquaintances, rivals indeed for the hand of Annetta. Although Rivers had been best man at the day's ceremony, he was deeply stricken with jealousy. As the ship headed out into the English Channel, he picked up a large wooden club and crushed the skull of the sailor at the ship's wheel. Taking the wheel himself, he steered straight for the Sands. The ship beached itself and in the high tides quickly flooded. Those below were trapped without any hope of escape.

The 'accident' was witnessed by passing boats and Rivers was heard to be laughing hysterically as the boat keeled over. All were drowned. At the inquest, Rivers' mother reluctantly testified that she had heard her son swear that one day he would get even with Reed.

That night's tragedy was only the beginning of the mystery. Every fifty years since on 13 February, sightings have been reported of a ghostly repeat of the grounding. In 1798 on this night, the *Edenbridge*, a coastal vessel, reported seeing a three-masted schooner coming straight towards it. The *Edenbridge*'s captain took evasive action to avoid a collision and, as the ship swept past, the sounds of merrymaking could be heard from below. The sighting was verified by another ship which reported seeing the same vessel proceed to beach itself on the Sands and break up before their eyes. Sailing to the scene to give assistance, they found nothing there.

On 13 February 1848, a number of ships out from Deal saw the ship marooned on the Sands. Again, a passing American ship, witnessing the apparent tragedy, sailed to the spot to assist but when it arrived there was nothing to be seen. In 1898, people on the shore this time reported the same three-masted schooner coming to grief but no tangible evidence could be found.

Regrettably, no account can be found for 1948, and by 1998 the whole affair had been so well forgotten that no one probably knew that there was anything strange to look for. But one for the diary for 2048.

AHOY – FANCY MEETING YOU HERE!

■ *One of the oddest marine accidents in history occurred off Dungeness. The mishap itself was unremarkable – there was no loss of life and neither ship was lost – but it deserves a place in the annals of Kent's curious disasters because of the one bizarre coincidence.*

The incident involved the coming together of two ships in dense fog just after 9.30 on the evening of 19 June 1909. One was a Royal Navy warship, HMS *Sappho*, that had left Portsmouth earlier in the morning bound for manoeuvres in Scapa Flow in the Orkneys. The other was a cargo ship coming in the opposite direction down from Hull heading for the Mediterranean. Conditions were treacherous in the extreme. In the neighbourhood of Dungeness Point ships were employing their sirens continuously and visibility was virtually zero.

It was less than a minute after first spotting her that the merchant ship crashed into the cruiser at precisely its weakest point, leaving a gaping hole beneath the water line adjacent to the engine room which was immediately flooded causing a complete loss of power and even electricity to power the radio. In the circumstances, it was nothing short of a miracle that no hands were lost.

A major rescue operation was launched from Dover and a flotilla of small boats took most of the 250 crew off. The cruiser was towed into Dover just in time before she partly sank. Oddly, the cargo ship that ploughed into the cruiser was hardly damaged and did not even need to put into port. After the collision the ship's owners received a telegram from the steamer reporting the accident, affirming that she had suffered no damage and that she was continuing on her course as planned! The warship – twice as big and supposedly built to defend an Empire – lay crippled and barely afloat!

The oddity about the affair deepened when it came to light that the cargo ship that had struck HMS *Sappho* was called ... the *Sappho*!

Given the number of vessels then afloat, the odds on the two ships ever passing in the night, let alone colliding with each other, must be astronomical. But enthusiasts of ancient Greek will have detected the greater irony lying inside this indiscreet mingling of these sister ships. Sappho was the 6th-century BC poetess from Lesbos whose encouragement of her fellow islanders for mutual love gave our language the word now used for those females who seek out others. Sappho herself would not have been a bit surprised.

'FIRE, HELP – SEND A TELEGRAM'

▣ *What must rank as one of the oddest documents ever produced in the county was rushed off on the evening of 4 October 1898 giving an insight into life in the villages as recently as a hundred years ago.*

It was a telegram, preserved in the archives of the local newspaper, which only came to light a century later when it was produced as part of the newspaper's centenary celebrations. It came from the village of Loose, about two miles south of Maidstone and it read, in all simplicity and urgency: 'To – Kent Fire Officer, Maidstone. Send fire engine church cottages Loose at once.'

Bizarrely, it was the quickest way to get a message in those days for many villages before telephones reached out beyond the towns. The fire in Loose had begun shortly before seven in the evening. According to the copy of the telegram preserved, the message was taken at Loose at 6.50 pm and took four minutes to get through to Maidstone. By the time the fire brigade arrived, villagers had brought the blaze under control, so the firemen, it was reported, promptly returned home without having to do anything.

It goes to show that anyone who took the risk of living further out than the even comparatively proximate people of Loose had essentially to fend for themselves.

THE LONGEST FIRE

■ *In 1952, a fire at a Northfleet paper mill set an unusual disaster record.*

Kent fire brigade's longest call-out ended on 11 August 1952 with the extinguishing of the last remnants of the blaze at the mill. The brigade could be forgiven for thinking at times that it would never go out. They had been on duty at the scene for an unprecedented stint – 32 days!

The emergency had begun way back on 11 July when 1,200 tons of esparto grass, used in the manufacture of paper and being stored in a warehouse at the mill, caught fire. It took crews a couple of hours to bring the main fire under control. As mill workers fought to salvage as much of the unburnt esparto as they could, smouldering hot spots of grass kept bursting into flames as they became exposed to the air by the raking process, requiring the fire crew to douse the area to prevent the blaze re-starting.

And so it went on, day by day, week by week, until, a calendar month later, the fire could finally, definitively and absolutely be declared out. Phew!

PERSONAL DISASTERS
■ *Among the strange deaths and near-death experiences recorded in Kent, these must rank as some of the weirdest personal tragedies imaginable.*

If at first you don't succeed ... (1)
... try again was clearly the motto of a suicide that is possibly the strangest taking of one's own life likely to have been recorded anywhere in Britain. On 31 August 1903 the Canterbury coroner held an inquest into the death by suicide of laundryman George Luff. It was a sad case indeed. He had attempted suicide the previous April, but unsuccessfully. At the resulting court case he had been handed into the care of his wife. That, the coroner said with hindsight, had evidently been a mistake. The man had now achieved his objective in the most astonishing of ways. He had taken a carpenter's saw and sawn through his own skull into his brain.

If at first you don't succeed ... (2)
Local papers reported in January 1947 the bizarre suicide effort of a 27-year-old Dartford labourer Donald Stonely who attempted to kill himself three times in a single night – and failed. Since attempted suicide was still a criminal offence, Stonely found himself facing a court trial where the comic details were comprehensively displayed for public consumption. He had been found by police apparently trying to freeze himself to death in the refrigerator of a butcher's shop in Dartford High Street.

As the background to the affair emerged, it became curiouser and curiouser. Stonely confessed to feeling depressed on the evening in question. This had been caused mainly by his waiting on a street corner for some time for his date before realising that he had been stood up. He decided at that point to kill himself and elected to jump off a nearby bridge into the river. When he got there he had second thoughts, chiefly, he said, because he could not swim – a strange consideration, perhaps – and anyway the water looked too cold, so he chose instead to jump off the nearest building – which happened to be the butcher's shop.

He climbed onto the roof and was making his way to the edge when he put his foot through a glass skylight, lost his balance and fell through the hole into the shop. Miraculously (but unfortunately for an aspiring suicide) he was still unscathed and at a loss to know how to get out. Realising it was a butcher's, he found his way to the refrigerator and climbed in.

'I knew if I stayed in the refrigerator, it would injure me,' he told West Kent Sessions Court. He was found, though, a short while later by two police officers investigating a possible break-in after a neighbour reported the sound of breaking glass. He was covered in ice but otherwise none the worse for his experience. Warmed up, he came before the court, which was told that he had had nine previous convictions for various offences and seven terms of imprisonment. The eventful night landed him another nine months inside.

Death in a bucket

A most peculiar death occurred in Saltwood, near Folkestone, in March 1938. The body of Dorothy Wall, a 29-year-old woman, was discovered by her husband on his return from work. She was lying on the kitchen floor with her head in a bucket of water. There were no other signs to indicate how she got there. At the inquest, the husband told how she had suffered for years from uncontrollable fits, presumably epilepsy. The court concluded that she must have been overcome by such a fit, fallen forward and caught her head in the bucket. She was officially recorded as having died by drowning in her own kitchen.

Run over by a train 12 times

This remarkable accident was reported by the police in October 1953. They described the man as probably the luckiest person alive. He had been found severely injured in the middle of the tracks on a remote railway bridge early on the morning of 2 October. He had, it seemed, survived being run over by a train during the night – not once, but twelve times!

The victim was established to be 43-year-old George Lesley but no one was yet any the wiser as to how or why he came to be on the viaduct at Eynsford. When he was found his injuries consisted of a severed foot, a partially severed other foot, serious head injuries and a fractured arm. Piecing together the story, it emerged that he had been on the tracks for eight hours. He told police he had lost count of the number of trains that had passed over him. The railway's records indicated that it had been at least a dozen.

Police had found a witness, a worker at a nearby water pumping station, who told them that around midnight on the night in question he had heard cries from the bridge, but he was 'used to hearing weird noises during the night so he did not attach any importance to them.' Six hours later, a railway worker heard the groans too and went onto the bridge and discovered Lesley. An approaching Victoria–Sevenoaks train was stopped on the line and the Eynsford stationmaster and a police officer ventured onto the viaduct to recover him. He was stretchered away and taken up to the station from where he was despatched by ambulance to Dartford. Railway officials remarked that despite the gravity of his injuries, he was still a miraculously lucky man. Had he moved his arms inches either way during his all-night ordeal, he would have been electrocuted by the live rails.

A report two days later said that Lesley's surviving foot had had to be amputated. Police had begun to interview him but he was refusing to reveal the background to his bizarre escapade. Unfortunately there is no further record of the case, other than a news report a fortnight later that doctors in the hospital had taken him off the danger list, so it will probably never be known whether it was an odd choice for a short cut or a suicide bid which did not come off. If the latter, Lesley probably acquires some sort of record for failing twelve consecutive attempts to take his life.

A miraculous escape

We conclude with a heart-warming vignette. Described as 'Kent's Luckiest Boy', 7-year-old Barry McGovarin astonished the country by being completely run over by a double-decker bus and emerging totally unscathed.

The accident happened in January 1947 as he made his way to school at Blue Town, Sheerness. He was tucking into an orange at the time, which his mother had carefully wrapped in a protective paper to stop his hands getting sticky. It was this that nearly killed him.

As he ate, the piece of paper blew away unhelpfully into the middle of the road. Thinking only about sticky fingers, he unhesitatingly went after it, bent down to retrieve it and lifted his head to see the double-decker about to hit him. With astonishing presence of mind, according to eyewitnesses, he threw himself flat on the road and the bus passed directly over him. The driver pulled up and while he and his conductor emerged rather shakily, the boy was crawling out from under the back of the bus without a scratch. The driver, who told the local press that he could have done nothing to swerve either side of the boy, said that the lad's only reaction was to plead 'not to be locked up for it' as he grinned and continued to finish off his orange.

He insisted on carrying on to school and told no one there of the incident. Only when his mother, who had been contacted by police, turned up at the school did the schoolmaster confess to thinking that the boy had looked 'a little colourless' that morning. The youngster was later reported to have given a demonstration of his action to officers at the local police station and the bus driver was last heard of suggesting that reports of the escape should be distributed to all schools in the county as a demonstration of how keeping one's head in dangerous situations pays off.